T0278500

The Contemporary Leader

The Contemporary Leader

The Value of Inclusion in Successful Leadership

Riza Kadilar

WILEY

This edition first published 2025

Riza Kadilar ©2025

Registered Office(s)
John Wiley & Sons, Inc., 111 River Street, Hoboken, NJ 07030, USA
John Wiley & Sons Ltd, The Atrium, Southern Gate, Chichester, West Sussex, PO19 8SQ, UK

Editorial Office
The Atrium, Southern Gate, Chichester, West Sussex, PO19 8SQ, UK

For details of our global editorial offices, customer services, and more information about Wiley products visit us at www.wiley.com.

Library of Congress Cataloging-in-Publication Data is Available:

ISBN 978-1-394-27637-0 (Hardback)
ISBN 978-1-394-27639-4 (ePDF)
ISBN 978-1-394-27638-7 (ePUB)

Cover Design: Wiley
Cover Image: © Dedraw Studio/Adobe Stock Photos
Author Photo: Courtesy of Riza Kadilar

SKY10089053_102524

Dedicated to

My family,
My late father, mother, brother,
My lovely wife and my beloved daughter,

For making me who I'm today and for the life you've given me.

Contents

Foreword

From **Unknown** to **Our Own**, From **Nothing** to **One**

> Accepting the other, the foreign, the different,
> and those not of your own just as they are;
> Forming an ideal union with those who are not
> from your circle, uniting;
> Reaching out wholeheartedly to what seems
> unreachable, distant, difficult, or unbelievable;
> Expanding, growing, flourishing, incorporating
> the external into the internal;
> Internalizing and together creating a value,
> granting existence;
> Understanding the excluded, noticing the
> barriers to exclusion;
> Welcoming the invitation, finding delight in it,
> feeling it as our own;
> Knowing you are seen and heard, being in a
> respectful and safe environment;
> Including and being included.

To realize all these, knowingly, willingly, consciously, aware of the costs and rewards, actively holding the reins of our lives in our hands. . .

Adorning such an approach, the purpose of this book is

- to accompany you on this journey,
- to support you in aligning your inner world with changing external conditions,
- and, all throughout this process, to help you better understand yourself, enhance the quality of your internal dialogue, and enable you to live in greater welfare and peace in a changing world.

Acknowledgements

There are so many people who have contributed to my encounter and confrontation with the concepts discussed in this book. Some have inspired me with their inclusive approaches, others with their exclusions. Ultimately, this book emerged from a lifetime of accumulated experiences.

Of course, the person most deserving of thanks is dear Günnur Kabasakal, who has brought together the very scattered pieces of this book and, with a meticulous editor's approach, shaped them into its current form. Günnur's effort is immense in assembling my hundreds of fragmented writings on these topics, transcribing hours of various speeches, summarizing them, and blending all these with additional resources to create this work. Special thanks goes as well to Tuğba Atamtürk, for her dedicated support for the final edit, and to Alperen Tekin for his diligent work on the English translation of the book.

I would also like to extend my thanks to dear Abide Tekelioğlu, Buse Gamze Leblebiciler, Gül Üstün, Hülya Paşaoğulları, Murat Özpehlivan, and Şeyda Bodur for their support during the final reading and review phase.

Linbert Spencer, who has introduced me to the concept of inclusion on an academic level, and dear Peter Hawkins and David Clutterbuck, who have enriched me intellectually through our lengthy discussions, also played a very significant role. Their wisdom inspired me since the very first day I met them.

I owe a lot to my family, Pelin and Kardelen, who have beautifully reflected and mirrored my personal relationship with the concept of inclusion and occasionally enhanced my awareness with their merciless comments. Their help in making me realize my own contradictions while advocating for truths in such a matter was an invaluable contribution to both me and this book you are holding in your hands.

And of course, I can never thank my late father and my dear mother enough, who have enriched my transforming personality during the childhood years with the paradigms, teachings, values, and love they have never withheld.

Taking on various roles in multicultural environments, especially being the president at EMCC Global; sometimes felling a part of a minority alongside other cultures; having lived in different countries; adorning my life with third cultures; and always being curious about multiple perspectives rather than just one were probably the other factors that have supported me on this journey.

I extend endless thanks to those in both my family and the educational world including all my elders, friends, and the young people who had an impact on me and those on whom I had the chance to create one.

Introduction

This book suggests that if a seed you have sown does not sprout as expected, the seed itself may not be at fault. Getting angry at the seed will not help. For a seed to grow, sprout, and bear fruit, it certainly requires certain inherent qualities, but perhaps more crucial is that it is placed in an environment conducive to its growth.

Every person, and indeed every human group, is akin to a seed. To develop and realize their potential, they need not only inherent qualities but also an environment that supports their growth.

This is what we mean by inclusion. The question we tackle is: How can we cultivate a living environment where diverse seeds, each with unique traits and distinctly different from one another, can sprout together and flourish sustainably?

This idea mirrors the natural cycle of our world where various life forms have evolved to coexist. Those unable to adapt have perished with time, while others have modified their traits to survive. Nature operates in cycles: the output of one process becomes the input for another until human intervention disrupted these cycles.

For example, mono-culture agriculture began with humans, extending over time not just as an agricultural method but also with its essence permeating social spheres. As Harari points out, the real strength which enabled *Homo sapiens* to become the rulers of this world lies in their ability to cooperate and organize collectively to tackle challenges and threats. Historically, societies that had excelled in this organization and cooperation achieved greater prosperity and dominance. They formed mono-culture communities, unified by similar belief systems, rituals, educational philosophies, and social and individual values, which enabled them to dominate not only other societies but also the geographies they inhabited. Concurrently, this homogeneity is why some of the greatest wars and destructions have unfolded throughout human history.

Today, however, this pattern need not persist. As this book meticulously details, societies composed of diverse individuals stand to gain significantly if they can foster a spirit of cooperation. This is due to a number of reasons, some of which range from the advancements in technology to demographic shifts, and the widespread sharing of diverse worldviews, especially from Asia. Such a scenario offers more than just benefits; as without fostering diversity and inclusion, we will also be facing some considerable risks. Artificial intelligence, for example, operates on learning algorithms (called machine learning) that evolve based on the data we feed them. Whatever we input into the system, that is, whatever we teach the algorithms, it further develops the applications in that direction. If we teach artificial intelligence that the mono-culture approach is the most effective solution available, we may end up leaving a terrible future for our children and grandchildren.

Inclusion, therefore, transcends being merely a fashionable term; it is a fundamentally vital, existential concept. Yet each concept inherently has its counter as well, and globally, particularly in political arenas, we observe a surge in divisive rhetoric. The outcome will depend on which approach we choose to nurture, and time is of the essence.

The recent pandemic serves as a prime example. A threat potent enough to potentially end humanity was swiftly mitigated with minimal damage, thanks to global scientific cooperation and the support of many. It underscored the remarkable and effective outcomes achievable when unified by a common goal. While the immediate threat has subsided, the experience has illuminated the beauty of living in a diverse society. The proverbial genie is out of the bottle, and it is now our responsibility to leverage these gains to develop even more effective solutions, although some may attempt to reverse this progress.

This book seeks to elucidate the promises of inclusion.

The first chapter explores the nature of inclusion and its recent emergence.

The second chapter discusses the link between inclusion, productivity (performance), and diversity, emphasizing not just diversity of perspectives but also psychological diversity and the diversity stemming from the stories of our varied backgrounds.

In the third chapter, we delve into leadership. Beginning with the current paradigms, we explore leadership qualities that embody the era and the concept of inclusion. This chapter also offers insights into my own personal approach to the aforementioned concepts in light of my experiences.

Subsequent chapters scrutinize concepts that enhance our capacity for inclusion or act as barriers to it:

a. We start with primary emotions. You must have heard the saying which asserts that "Humans are rational beings". While it is true that humans are rational, we are also predominantly emotional beings who occasionally engage in thought. The important thing is to notice and recognize our emotions and to make them functional. So this is where we start.

b. Next, we focus on the critical concept of empathy.

c. We then analyse the concept of trust and trust in the psychological sense.

As for the barriers:

d. We first examine unconscious biases, associations, and cognitive dissonances.

e. Next, we assess how our privileges can hinder the processes of inclusion.

f. We then scrutinize our exclusions.

g. The concepts of invisibility and being excluded are discussed subsequently.

h. Finally, we address the concept of belonging.

After considering environmental factors, just as with the need for seeds to possess certain qualities to grow as we have discussed in the beginning, we proceed to discuss individual development processes and the significance of a growth mindset. Growth encompasses embracing new experiences and insights previously unincorporated. In this sense, inclusion plays a crucial role in these individual development processes.

Of course, development is important not only at the individual level but also at the institutional level. For institutional development to be achieved, again, our inclusion capacity needs to grow. In the following section, we first suggest a measurement tool for our institutions, followed by a recommended strategic development model for institutional inclusion.

In the eighth chapter of the book, we explore key areas that can inspire us or find practical application within the realm of inclusion.

First of all, we delve into topics inspired by Japanese culture.

We then address the issue of women's employment, a significant topic in our country, through the lens of the Athena Doctrine.

We discuss the concept of resilience, the Gestalt approach to change management, the applications in coaching, the mentoring approach, along with the theory of situational leadership, and the concept of the "Four Horsemen" which perhaps encapsulates the most significant barriers to functional cooperation and teamwork. And finally, recognizing the growing significance of data science, we include a set of recommendations from the perspective of a data scientist, intended to be passed on to future generations.

Of course, the book does not truly end there. Each topic briefly touched upon here will be discussed more thoroughly through the RK Academy portals which will also include additional resources. We envision this book as the start of a new journey in furthering your personal development.

Why a Book on This Topic and Why Now?

Humanity is at a pivotal juncture. We face a choice: learn to live and produce together with those who differ from us, building a new tomorrow, or allow the current process of polarization to usher us into an era rife with some of the greatest disasters in human history. By "different", I refer not only to communities with distinct beliefs, preferences, perspectives, and life cycles but also to abstract concepts unfamiliar to us. New discourses which contradict those we assume to be true, new perspectives that make us question the paradigms we classify as good and new ways and manners to live – all these fall within the scope of this concept.

Saying "Let's be inclusive", unfortunately, is not enough. I observe so often that almost everyone uses the term "inclusion" as if merely stating it would make it a reality. It does not. Because the anthropological, sociological, community genetics, and psychological reflexes and habits we have developed over history prevent this. Human communities have historically suffered greatly from differences. Wars, invasions, revolutions, and social turmoil have all stemmed from them. Not only different lifestyles, belief systems, and economic needs but also the emergence of new and different concepts have put people under social stress. Sometimes blood has been shed within families. Human history is replete with such dramas. Consequently, a deep-seated aversion to, exclusion of, and self-protection from the dissimilar have been ingrained in the human brain – situated centrally, powerfully, and close to our survival instincts.

However, we now recognize that this must change due to technological, demographic, and sociological reasons. This book has been written for this purpose. A common motivation among those who speak and convey any topic is perhaps to heal. Whether it is to solve a problem, invent tools, discover methods, or alleviate pain, to be more successful . . . Whatever the issue, we share the solutions we find with our loved ones with the intention of healing. As such, this work was born from my desire to share recent developments and the solutions I have discovered regarding inclusion and inclusive leadership.

Inclusion is easy to proclaim but challenging to internalize and practice.

Discussing inclusion in a homogeneous society, all similar in shape and colour, is not meaningful because if we have built a fortress composed of "the same" and are content there, isolated and disconnected from the outside, then discussing inclusion serves no purpose. Inclusion is an emotional state which only truly emerges when the fortress walls are torn down; when very different people, perspectives and beliefs come together; and when different lifestyles permeate every aspect of our lives.

Inclusion stands as one of the most important answers of our time, capable of addressing the most critical of questions. It also serves as a tool to rectify the problems embedded within these questions. Of course, this does not mean it can solve all life's problems. Inclusion is merely one of the keys to success, happiness, health, and peace in our world. I believe that the new methods and approaches facilitated by this mindset will lead us to a far more prosperous place. So keep in mind that the perspectives shared throughout this work should be considered from this viewpoint.

I still experience exclusion daily or rediscover aspects of life which I exclude. There are areas in life where I feel no need to include, yet I recognize the cost of such exclusions. And that is, essentially, what I wish to convey: to recognize the cost.

Reflecting on my past, I can assert that I was a diligent student. I could anticipate the questions that might be asked and how to answer them; my understanding of patterns has helped me navigate both educational and professional environments more effectively. Throughout this work, maintaining the diligence from my school years, I share useful methods and experiences that I have developed in response to life's challenges. Rather than accepting these as given, I encourage you to consider how they might be integrated into your life.

Only you can truly understand where the methods and the philosophy of inclusion I advocate can address or mitigate the deficiencies in our lives. You should focus on areas that will minimize your costs and facilitate overcoming challenges. Reflect on your truths and your lives; consider which aspects of the work you can incorporate that could be of use to you. No one else can know the emotions you experience, but within the pages of this book, you may end up finding something supportive.

So am I inclusive enough? Frankly, I must confess that while working on this book, I have realized that the thought patterns, emotional ties, conscious and unconscious biases, and especially the privileges I have strived to attain in life made me quite an excluding individual. And as it turns out, many of the difficulties I have faced in leadership roles had stemmed from these unknowingly developed approaches. Yet, was becoming aware of this sufficient? Of course not. It is a crucial step to recognize. But next, one needs to accept that this is a problem. I have completed this step as well. But the real challenge begins only afterwards. The process of achieving this change must be approached very consciously and consistently. In this process, many of the tools mentioned in the book have proved invaluable for me too. Change does not happen overnight. I embarked on this journey consciously, willingly, and persistently, and I have already seen significant benefits. In fact, even before this book was published, it seems to have provided the greatest benefit to its own author . . .

I would like to provide some fundamental questions to consider on the course of this journey:

- What do I choose to exclude, and what is the cost of these exclusions for me?
- How do I manage its burden?
- What aspects of this bring me happiness?
- Can I continue with the truths I have established so far?
- Who am I as a leader?
- What does this leadership role mean to me?
- What aspects of leadership appeal to me?
- Where do I come from, and where am I heading?
- What is the meaning of life to me?

To reiterate, inclusion is an easy-to-articulate but challenging-to-practice philosophy. In many ways, it challenges our established truths and the lives we lead.

• • •

We are in an era of unprecedented technological change and development. We are at the forefront of algorithms, processes, and methods that could build spaceships as large as planets, previously depicted only in science fiction films. There are incredibly innovative learning opportunities like machine learning, deep learning, and fast learning.

If we transmit flawed truths into learning systems such as these, we will see the errors proliferate very fast. "Garbage in, garbage out", as they say. If we input our biases, exclusions, stereotypes, or divisions into the system as they are, we may witness all of these multiplying and potentially creating an uninhabitable world.

The message here is clear. We must move away from the truths that have brought us here and discover new paradigms; only then can we input useful and inclusive truths into machines that learn quickly.

When future generations find the studies on inclusion and inclusive leadership which we are currently conducting, it might, I imagine, bring a smile to their faces in remembrance of us.

We do not yet know where all this is going. I am merely striving to formulate a response with the reflex of a student who knows how to give the right answer.

It is my hope that upon finishing this book, you will not hesitate to revisit this topic.

1

Why Inclusion and Why Now?

What Do We Mean by Inclusion?

In today's world, diversity and inclusion have become two of the most important concepts for the business world on a global scale. You might wonder, "With all the challenges, threats, and difficulties we face, why is such a humane issue so prominent on the agenda?" In this section, I aim to explain that inclusion is indeed an antidote to many of today's challenges. This means that if humanity is to surmount the obstacles it currently faces, it will only be through the actions of inclusive leaders and the culture of inclusion they are to promote. We begin with this bold assertion.

Throughout human history, societies that organized most efficiently and implemented the most effective cooperation among their individuals have proven to be stronger and more successful against natural elements and other human communities. This advantage has consistently been facilitated more easily through social norms. Yet we recognize that homogeneous structures are significantly more vulnerable to changing conditions. For instance, genetic diversity strengthens human communities against biological and ecological threats. Likewise, diversity in gender, culture, age, geography, and academic disciplines, when synergistically integrated, enhances the resilience of institutions against economic threats. Factors like the rapid pace of change, along with ecological, technological, and geopolitical threats, and digitalization, underscore the benefits of greater diversity within institutions and human communities. In this context, diversity efforts are becoming increasingly vital. However, if individuals with differing characteristics cannot coexist harmoniously, the resulting diversity might cause more destruction rather than success. The answer lies in fostering inclusion and practicing inclusive leadership. Inclusion is defined as a social and psychological state where each individual feels valued, acknowledged, safe, and trusted; experiences a sense of belonging; and can perform at their best – it is a state of feeling which sets it apart from action-oriented concepts like equality and diversity.

Inclusion is defined as a social and psychological state where each individual feels valued, acknowledged, safe, and trusted; experiences a sense of belonging; and can perform at their best.

An inclusive environment fosters warm, trust-based human relationships and encourages sharing, curiosity, contribution, transparency, and the impulse to excel. It also thrives on justice, equity, mutual respect, responsibility, appreciation and being appreciated, collaboration, and the shared experience of success.

To What Change Does Inclusion Owe Its Current Importance?

There's a saying I find quite resonant: "Partnerships are not made by partners but through common goals". This adage underscores that creating an inclusive climate is more attainable for organizations that rally around shared objectives and place their primary mission at the forefront.

As Simon Sinek emphasizes in *Start with Why*,[1] "institutions driven by purpose" (a popular term nowadays), where differences align with common goals and visions, foster environments conducive to inclusion. In these organizations, leaders act as facilitators of common goals. We observe that inclusive leadership, particularly in multicultural workplaces, significantly boosts harmony among employees and enhances productivity.

> **Inclusive leadership, especially in multicultural workplaces, enhances both harmony and productivity among employees.**

The increasing significance of inclusion and inclusive leadership perspective is propelled by numerous factors. Among these are the importance of labour unity in societal and historical contexts, advancements in basic sciences, and emerging social developments.

Innovations in Basic Sciences and Social Developments

History lessons have often taught us that it was the great leaders and the pivotal events around them which had shaped our history. Yet there may also be another crucial layer underlying history which involves advancements in the field of science. Innovations in agriculture and military technologies, followed by breakthroughs in basic and later social sciences over the last century, have all played a significant role. Viewing human history through the lens of these developments offers a more effective method to understand the leadership qualities required in each era.

Numerous examples abound, from the invention of the wheel and firearms to the herring fish being caught and salted on open seas, enabling fleets to navigate for months without docking. Innovations such as antibiotics, the telescope, the compass, Cartesian thought, electricity, quantum mechanics, and the internet have all facilitated new understandings of leadership in the years that followed. One of the more subtle examples might be the change in the social status of women. The now-widely-accepted egalitarian practices of our day can partly be attributed to the discovery and widespread use of birth-control pills. When women gained control over their destinies, they also began to break free from their historically prescribed roles in social and economic arenas. This list of influential developments can be extended even further.

Which Scientific Advancements Have Triggered the Progress We Are Now Experiencing in Inclusion?

The questions that arise are numerous. What were these cutting edge technological developments of such importance?

What shapes our current understanding of leadership today and will continue to influence it in the near future?

While there is not a single definitive answer, some notable examples include neural networks, genetics-supported neuroscience, quantum mechanics, GPS, and new approaches in sociology and psychology. To delve deeper into this discussion.

The most pivotal development in this regard has been the change in our perspective on the theory of evolution through what might be termed as "multilevel selection" (MLS) theory. Secondly, there are the academic contributions of Elinor Ostrom, the recipient of the Nobel Prize in economics for the year 2009, finding areas of practical application both in societal life and in the business world.

Darwin's theory of evolution, although now controversially positioned by Huxley's contributions, initially provided a robust framework for understanding life on Earth and the development of species. Darwin based his theory on three fundamental elements:

- Measurable characteristics of living organisms that change over generations.
- These changes providing them with an advantage in their environment in terms of their survival and the continuation of their lineage.
- The transmission of these changes to future generations.

When these three elements converge, the evolutionary development process as described by Darwin comes to life, gradually becoming a general characteristic of the species.

While this theory effectively explains the development of certain vital characteristics, it does not adequately account for the formation and evolution of social behaviours, moral norms, and societal traditions across generations. Traits such as respect, devotion, politeness, honesty, trust, courage, and even altruism often do not provide an advantage to the individual and may even place them at a disadvantage. Even in modern society, let alone throughout history, these traits do not necessarily offer individuals a survival advantage over selfish, self-centred individuals. So how did these traits develop over time to reach us today, and how have they come to prominence within the concept of "inclusion" that we will extensively discuss in this book?

Yuval Harari, in his book *Sapiens*, suggests that our ancestors' ability to dominate other "homo" species was due to their superior organization and cooperation within their communities. Similarly, where Darwin's theory meets challenges, he touches on the concepts of "individual evolution" and "social evolution". That is, while the aforementioned traits may disadvantage the individuals exhibiting them, the communities displaying these traits gain an advantage over other communities, supporting the three elements of evolution. While selfish, self-centred individuals may have a competitive edge, history shows that communities that foster cooperation and protect communal interests have been more advantageous.

Another key reason this topic is included in this book is the concept of natural selection, which initially starts in smaller communities and gradually expands to larger ones on a scale from the individual to the entirety of humanity where smaller communities eventually form the larger versions. The technological advancements and their facilitation of more effective demographic movements have transformed what was once a social evolution confined to families, villages, tribes, local communities, or even nations and races into a broader phenomenon through the interaction of larger communities. In other words, while the characteristics of a neighbouring village or country were once elements in evolutionary competition, today we are witnessing a process where subcultures around the world are competing with each other.

Of course, the phenomenon we call evolution manifests through changes observed over generations. It is not yet feasible to discern how the dramatic developments of the last century, unprecedented in history, will evolutionarily impact humanity. Here, science aids our understanding. When discussing social traits, we inevitably explore what can be learned from other organisms. A study conducted by Purdue University academic William Muir serves as an inspiration for us to underscore the importance of "inclusion" in MLS with regard to our future. In the experiment, initially, chicks from the most fertile chickens and roosters were selected to breed the next generation. This approach, when continued over five generations, resulted in a significant decline in egg production. The experiment was then repeated, but with a focus on selecting the most productive groups of chickens rather than the most productive individuals. This approach means that instead of focusing on individual champions, the process allowed a small group that had outperformed others to form the next generation. As anticipated, this group selection approach did not decrease but increased egg production in subsequent generations. It turns out, individual performance, which presumably favoured traits prioritizing personal over communal interests, did not lead to more productive communities. Conversely, communities formed by individuals who prioritized communal interests not only thrived collectively but also left a better legacy for their future generations.[2]

If such results emerge from chickens, might similar principles apply to human communities?[3] An experiment involving university students in America provides some insight.

In this study, students who have just started their education in the university were chosen and assessed for their propensity to help others with a test. Months later, the same assessment was repeated with the same students who were now asked to share the test questions with two friends of their choice. Subsequently, these students and their two friends were called to participate in a competitive game where the winners received free movie tickets. At the game's conclusion, students who had been identified as more individualistic and self-interested won more tickets individually. However, when evaluated as groups, those who had been initially tested as more altruistic collectively won more tickets with the two friends they have invited. While this experiment does not incorporate an evolutionary component, it also does not yield drastically different results from the chicken experiment, reinforcing the naturally advantageous positions of communities formed by individuals who prioritize social values. The experiment also highlights the importance of inclusion in both contemporary and evolutionary contexts.

Homo Economicus

Another significant and more contemporary development is found in the works of Nobel Prize recipient economist Elinor Ostrom. Ostrom's research indicated that both centralized structures and market mechanisms, such as privatization, fall short in managing situations involving common, scarce resources that should benefit everyone. She demonstrated that groups capable of self-organization could effectively address these challenges. Economists, traditionally toggling between centralized decisions and market mechanisms, were introduced by Ostrom to a third, viable solution.

Ostrom's contributions are particularly significant as they offer hope for resolving critical global issues like the management of natural resources – forests, oceans, and water.

To understand Ostrom's work, we should first refer to an article that inspired her. In 1968, the year I was born, ecologist Garrett Hardin published an article in *Science* magazine. Hardin's piece presented the following scenario:

> *Picture a pasture open to all. It is to be expected that each herdsman will try to keep as many cattle as possible on the commons. Such an arrangement may work reasonably satisfactorily for centuries because tribal wars, poaching, and disease keep the numbers of both man and beast well below the carrying capacity of the land. Finally, however, comes the day of reckoning, that is, the day when the long-desired goal of social stability becomes a reality. At this point, the inherent logic of the commons remorselessly generates tragedy. (. . .) The rational herdsman concludes that the only sensible course for him to pursue is to add another animal to his herd. And another; and another ... But this is the conclusion reached by each and every rational herdsman sharing a commons. Therein is the tragedy. Each man is locked into a system that compels him to increase his herd without limit – in a world that is limited. Ruin is the destination toward which all men rush, each pursuing his own best interest in a society that believes in the freedom of the commons. Freedom in a commons brings ruin to all.*

Ostrom's work demonstrated that centralized, top-down structures are ineffective at solving this paradox. In such systems, decision-makers either see themselves as outside of the system or exempt from the same rules and consequences, which are significant issues. Her research also showed that market solutions like privatization fail to deliver benefits, especially since market players are primarily motivated to maximize benefits for stakeholders rather than conserving resources, highlighting why market mechanisms are not a solution, as outlined by the classic agency problem in economic theory.

Ostrom's true achievement was proposing a new method in place of these ineffective theories. She showed that communities capable of self-organizing among their members and working functionally in cooperation with other similar human communities were viable and that only such systems could offer solutions to some of humanity's most significant challenges.

Ostrom's empirical studies laid out a clear method for how such communities function. She consolidated her doctoral thesis completed in 1965 and subsequent research into an article of pioneering quality in the field of economics, titled *Governing the Commons*, which was published in 1990 and has become one of the most referenced works in her field over the last two decades. The article introduced a new approach to the literature, known as "Ostrom's Law".

As I have mentioned earlier in this chapter, I believe that the major events in human history – political, economic, and technological developments – have been propelled by advances in the scientific field. The manifestation of Darwin's theory of evolution in the form of MLS theory in the social dimension, and following that, Ostrom's economic theory of self-organizing human communities and how they can solve major problems, together help us understand more deeply why the issue of inclusion is becoming increasingly important today.

So How Does All This Connect to Our Topic?

Ostrom's research indicates that communities structured around certain principles, known as "core design principles", might be our hope against the type of tragedy described by Hardin. These principles are as follows:

- Is the community clearly defined? Do members know that they are part of a group, what the group is about, and who is a member of this group without a state of ongoing debate?
- Are there locally adapted rules that equitably balance benefits and costs among members?
- Are collective choice arrangements in place allowing everyone affected by a decision to participate in making that decision?
- Are there monitoring systems capable of detecting deviations from agreed-upon behaviours? Is such a monitoring process being conducted – ideally – by group members and not external authorities?
- Are there graduated sanctions? Meaning, are deviations from behaviours addressed initially in a mild manner but with the possibility of escalating responses if needed?
- Are there mechanisms for resolving conflicts quickly in a manner deemed fair by all members?
- Is there a minimal recognition of organized rights, granting group members the authority to manage their own affairs without external interference, contrary to top-down regulation?
- Finally, can a polycentric governance occur when dealing with larger common-pool resources?

The emergence of these structures, described by and known as "the theory of polycentric governance", facilitates the development of self-governing communities, in the end, leading us to the concept of inclusion. We are discussing a system that must be nourished by values such as in-group respect, trust, reciprocity, and a sense of belonging, which are also fundamental to the concept of inclusion.

To summarize, humanity has perhaps really reached a critical juncture in its journey. Our planet may no longer be able to sustain us, and unfortunately, we are very close to the tragedy Hardin described. More importantly, the systems built thus far upon the theory of economics developed by humanity will not shield us from this tragedy. In this context, Ostrom's Nobel Prize–winning work offers us a ray of hope. We must foster inclusive societies to realize this hope.

Developments in Communications and Everyday Technology

"May you live in interesting times", goes a Chinese proverb. In fact, throughout human history, "interesting" and "curious" times have been recurring themes. I believe what is meant here is how individuals perceive the changes occurring around them with regard to being "interesting". Some changes have been purely destructive, such as wars and natural disasters. On the other hand, there are changes that signify a kind of "metamorphosis". Therefore, the significance of the process could be more about the individual's interpretation, rather than the process itself.

It is evident that new and advanced technologies have triggered disruptive transformations in various sectors. These technologies, termed "disruptive", also carry innovative features. In such an era, an individual's awareness, preparedness, and ability to leverage opportunities are crucial.

The phenomenon of digital transformation, often referred to as "uberization", has already made significant impacts across many sectors. We are witnessing a global reality known as "hub economies". The changes induced by the world's largest platforms affect us all, both as consumers and as professionals. It is useful to look at global examples in this context:

- The world's largest taxi company, Uber, does not have a single taxi on its balance sheet.
- The largest accommodation companies, both Airbnb and Booking.com, do not own any real estate chains or hotel rooms.
- The most used communication channels like Skype and WeChat do not own any telecommunication infrastructure.
- One of the largest retail companies, Alibaba, does not hold any inventory.
- A company we might call one of the largest in the media sector, namely Meta, does not produce content.
- The owner of the largest film collection, Netflix, does not have a movie theatre.
- The largest software sellers, Apple or Google, do not write the code of the applications they sell.

As evident, a tremendous transformation is occurring in the business world. Digital applications which were firstly created for enhancing operational efficiency then progressed to integrate social media, and they are now creating significant impact on payment systems and customer interactions in various sectors, as evident in every area of interaction between banks and their customers. When visiting a bank's website, one might not realize the presence of hundreds of startups behind it. Thousands of companies, most younger than five years, are now steering the customer relations of many banks. The processes related to personal banking and branch management, which currently constitute two-thirds of the costs of banks, are rapidly evolving. Some studies predict that one-third of bank jobs will disappear within seven years.

However, the primary unrecognized threat comes from technology leaders themselves. Previously grouped under FinTech, the term has gradually morphed into "TechFin". Payment systems, along with the savings and credit-related products developed by tech giants like Amazon, Google, Apple, and Microsoft, are set to shape the future of the financial sector. There are also intriguing developments in the automotive sector.

Particularly in China, the three musketeers known as "the BATs" (Baidu, Alibaba, Tencent) are increasingly forming partnerships with automotive industry leaders. In a world where autonomous vehicles are becoming a reality, the real competition is believed to focus on what passengers do inside the car, more specifically the apps they will use. Consequently, car manufacturers will perhaps need to prepare for a future where their revenue may not come from the cars themselves but from the software applications used within those cars.

A similar shift is occurring in the airline industry. Planes capable of staying airborne for nearly 20 hours and flying non-stop from one end of the world to the other are now operational. Direct, non-stop flights from London to Perth (Australia) have started, and direct flights from Singapore to New York have also begun to resume. How this development will affect hubs like İstanbul and Dubai, which have come to the forefront as transfer points for flights, is one aspect of the matter. More interestingly, the real competition in air travel will now shift towards service quality inside the aircraft rather than the distance the planes can fly. Factors like cabin lighting and air conditioning, jet-lag-friendly meals, and seat comfort will start to become the key determinants of passenger habits.

At the core of all these technological advancements, a fundamental truth stands out: your focus shapes your reality. In today's world, there is an increasingly apparent fact that the most valuable commodity has become people's "time and attention". Time or attention alone is not enough, but those who manage to attract both have become the ones who end up billing the most. The phrase "pay attention" includes the word "pay" in it after all, and it serves as a reminder to us that we can no longer ignore the inherent truth within the saying. The fiercest battles are now being fought over where to draw people's attention and time.

Industry players within the same sector are ceasing to become competitors to one another. For instance, when the CEOs of a leading Swiss watchmaker were hosting me in Geneva, they have indicated that their main competitors for prime retail spaces, where they are willing to pay top dollar in rent, were no longer the other watchmakers or jewellers. They are now losing these most prestigious of locations to brands like Apple, Nespresso, and Tesla.

Meanwhile, the discourse around artificial intelligence continues to evolve.

A digital transformation study by Fujitsu, involving thousands of companies from 14 countries, revealed some thought-provoking insights:

- 70% of participants expressed concern about their ability to adapt to artificial intelligence.
- 90% of business leaders participating in the study are taking steps to increase their access to digital expertise.

A study by KPMG, a leading global provider of audit, tax, and advisory services, revealed the following data:

- 80% of participants say their business models are changing due to disruptive technologies.
- 60% of participants are optimistic that disruptive technologies will create opportunities in their sectors.

What implications do these transformations hold for business leaders? How can we adapt to these developments, accelerating both our teams and the way we do business? To ignite further discussion, I would like to introduce my opinions on several topics.

The first one is awareness. We can initiate this reflective process by addressing the following questions in a sincere manner:

- How is digital transformation influencing my life, and which aspects do I view as threatening?
- Which of my attitudes and behaviours can be seen as resistance? What does my resistance tell me?
- Which values and goals does this resistance serve?
- Can I manage my personal digital transformation process better if I feel or do something differently by leveraging this resistance, and if so what is it?

Another concept I would like to highlight is "multi-stakeholder network management". It is evident that the traditional "boss says, employee does" approaches have become outdated. Yes, I am aware that the business world I have mainly worked for, and even the majority of the world still operates this way. However, times are changing.

The old order may still prevail in economies undergoing transformation across poverty-stricken regions and for routine, low-value-added jobs; however, it is beneficial to accept that life does not function in the same manner when considering high-value-added jobs. We must now ensure that individuals, over whom we have almost no coercion, contribute as we want them to, in order for us to achieve our desired outcome. This applies to corporate settings, commerce, academia, and even to families. We are moving beyond the "head of the family" debates. Today, our achievements are gauged by the outcomes of those within a multi-stakeholder network and over whom we have no direct control.

While the status quo is as such on the human side of things, there is also the concept of "big data". Professor Harari, speaking at Davos, explained, "In the twentieth century, democracies outperformed dictatorships, the most important reason behind this was because democracies facilitated data processing from multiple centres". In other words, he attributes the difference between democracies and autocracies to the existence of multi-centred versus single-centred mechanisms of data processing and decision-making. Further, he contends, "The capabilities of our day mean that the data collected and processed can enable more effective decisions when coming from a single centre".

Recent debates surrounding Cambridge Analytica and Facebook underscore Harari's warnings about digital dictatorships. We are led to believe that algorithms, which know us through a hundred likes on our social profiles, understand us better than we do ourselves. What this means is that we are living in an era where maintaining a heightened awareness and consciousness of "big data" and platform economies is crucial.

The current reality is that learning machines are going beyond human capabilities. Rarely can a human alone outperform machines. The era in which humans were outplayed by DeepMind in a game of Go marked a point of no return. On the other hand, if you were to add a collaborative group of people to the equation and support them with a learning machine, the outcome does change. In other words, collaboration between people equipped with both cognitive and human skills can promise us victorious teams.

Reflecting on the developments discussed earlier in the terms of inclusion, it is evident that technology plays a critical role in various aspects. In short and first of all, technology now enables personalized solutions across nearly every field. The manufacturing industries have attained the flexibility required to become as much customer-centric as the service sector. Finding individual-focused solutions is now feasible within acceptable cost frameworks across nearly all fields of business. Naturally, the same solutions are also evident in the realm of employee experience. Flexibility in workplaces provides individual-oriented solutions without significant cost burdens.

The second effect of technology is observed in business practices and economic models. The prevailing business model across numerous sectors has evolved into platform and market economies. It is no longer solely about the producer or consumer, sales and marketing, logistics or even operational excellence; rather, it is the platforms that amalgamate all of these aspects that are able to dominate business life, all the while creating unparalleled added value.

As a consequence, the definition of a brand is transforming. Historically, a brand was defined as "a promise made and the trust that the promise will be kept". Presently, it is the emotions associated with this trust, which significantly influence a brand's value as perceived by employees, customers, and investors. Therefore, the old adage "There is no room for emotions in trade" has been supplanted by "Shared emotions are now among the fundamental elements of business life".

The third notable impact of technology pertains to artificial intelligence. I would like to emphasize this: we are actually still very far away from truly discussing artificial intelligence. On the other hand, applications of machines such as deep learning (*machine learning*) and learning algorithms are nearly ubiquitous in every aspect of life.

> **It is unlikely that your job will be taken by a robot anytime soon. However, it is probable that you could lose your job to someone who is more adept at working alongside robots.**

Demographic Mobility

Nowadays, demographic mobility has reached unprecedented levels. Historically, large cities were the main hubs of human gatherings. However, the trend of dying in one's city of birth is decreasing, while the number of people relocating to different cities or countries continues to rise, fostering a melting pot of various cultures within countries, cities, and even subcultures.

For example, flights from Adana to İzmir in Türkiye, which were previously non-existent, have now become available and even direct. Many young people from Adana go to İzmir for university, perhaps finding jobs. Such demographic movements are now much more frequent than before. Means of transportation and the existence of new business opportunities are in the process of spreading chain platform economies to many more places. The same applies to various remote regions in countries like France, UK, and Eastern Europe. With such direct links, mutual relations have enormously evolved during the last two decades.

The scenario is similar globally. There is a significant brain drain and migration from Asia to the world's leading nations. This presents challenges for inclusion as diversity facilitates separation, differentiation, and stratification. Those who can harmoniously work together and embrace different cultures are increasingly prominent because the available human resources are now demographically diverse across subcultures.

The Global Rise and Spread of Asian and Eastern Cultures

The driving forces behind the push for inclusion are not merely human emotions or universal values, although these are some of the essential underpinnings. The real catalysts are new models of economics and business which are propelled by technological advancements, while the ascendancy of Asia also factors in.

Western enlightenment is based on a lifestyle and philosophy centred around the individual. For example, verb conjugations in all Western languages start with "I".

For years, we shared messages in leadership trainings along the lines of "The most important leader in your life is you". When Generation X was growing up, superheroes were the "Supermen" who defeated the villains alone and saved the world all by themselves. However, you might have noticed that in the most popular movies, superheroes now fight as teams. The one who ends up alone eventually loses. This narrative shift conveys a hidden message, particularly resonant for success in the Chinese market. We are increasingly feeling the impact of Asian societies that bring the concept of "we" to the forefront instead of "I". Concepts such as "Guan xi", "Ren qing", and "Mian zi"[4] are critical in understanding these shifts. They actually give us clues about employee experience and establishing a collaborative environment among individuals.

With the Eastern lifestyle becoming more prevalent in the entertainment sector, there is a transition from Europe's individualistic and Cartesian culture to a more holistic and comprehensive one. I do not want to delve into pondering about whether these constitute causes or effects. Such indications also reveal some major trends taking place in the world. As we have mentioned before, this process has ties with technology as well. Machine learning has now surpassed humans in almost every field. However, there are many examples of numerous people joining together and emerging triumphant over the machines.

To summarize:

There are some mega trends among the fundamental reasons of why the concept of inclusion has become so important that are beyond the perspective of "Humanity has reached a certain level of evolution and maturity, so let us love people". As outlined earlier, these include the advances in basic sciences and technology, demographic shifts, and the renewed interaction between Eastern and Western cultures.

"Why has inclusion become so important in the business world specifically?" Several studies provide insight into this question, and I would like to list some of them here:

According to a study by Korn Ferry,[5] organizations that correctly implement diversity as compared to their competitors achieve

- 70% faster growth and introduction of new ideas to the market
- 36% more profitability. and
- 87% better decision-making ability.

The same study suggests that inclusive leaders should exhibit traits such as the following:

- Authenticity
- Emotional resilience
- An optimistic self-determination
- Empathetic curiosity
- Flexibility

The prominent characteristics of inclusive organizations include the following:

- Establishing trust-based relationships between individuals
- Integrating different perspectives
- Evaluating talents as effectively as possible
- Applying an adaptive mindset
- Succeeding in transformation

A study by Deloitte[6] outlines the traits found in inclusive leaders as follows:

- Curiosity
- Cultural intelligence
- Collaboration
- Determination
- Courage
- Judgment

An article[7] published in the March 2020 issue of *Harvard Business Review* (*HBR*) lists the traits found in inclusive leaders as follows:

- Visible commitment and dedication
- Humility
- Awareness of biases
- Curiosity regarding others
- Cultural intelligence
- The ability of effective collaboration

Notes

1. Simon Sinek, Transl. Sevgi Şen, Neden ile Başla, Arıtan Publishing, 2022.
2. For further reading: Muir, W. M. (1985). "Relative efficiency of selection for performance of birds housed in colony cages based on production in single bird cages". *Poultry Science*, 64 (12), 2239–2247.
3. Muir, W.M. (1996). "Group selection for adaptation to multiple-hen cages: selection program and direct responses". *Poultry Science*, 75 (4), 447–458.

4. Sheldon, K.M., Sheldon, M.S., & Osbaldiston, R. (2000). "Prosocial values and group assortation: within an N-person prisoner's dilemma". *Human Nature*, 11 (4), 387–404.

5. To summarize briefly, "Guan xi" can be described as belonging to a group, acting as part of a society, carrying responsibility, and receiving support; "Ren qing" involves interpersonal relationships, the emotional distance that connects individuals, courtesy, respect, and establishing communication in mutual harmony; and "Mian zi" means not embarrassing anyone within the society, not causing someone to lose face or feel humiliated.

6. See https://www.kornferry.com/insights/articles/the-inclusive-leader (Date accessed: 09.10.2022).

7. See https://www2.deloitte.com/us/en/insights/topics/talent/six-signature-traits-of-inclusive-leadership.html (Date accessed: 09.10.2022).

8. See https://hbr.org/2020/03/the-key-to-inclusive-leadership

2

The Relationship Between the Concepts of Inclusion, Productivity, and Diversity

Performance and Productivity, and Inclusion

In the realm of inclusion, I had the valuable opportunity to collaborate with and learn from Linbert Spencer OBE, who has developed the following mathematical formula based on the factors affecting individual performance in business life:

$$P = (k + s + j) \, a^t$$

This formula consists of the initials of the following words:

- P: performance, profit
- k: knowledge
- s: skills, competencies
- j: judgement

In fact, both during our formal education years and in our professional lives, our focus has primarily been on the elements within the parentheses part of this formula. If someone possessed the adequate knowledge, has honed the necessary skills, and could apply these with sound judgement, what more could be necessary?

Then again, what do the "a" and "t" in the formula signify? A valid question. Because if the "a" equals zero, then the collective value of knowledge, skills, and judgement drops to zero, and if the "t" is negative, then the total value of all that knowledge, skill, and judgement ability turns into something much, much less in terms of performance.

According to the formula, the "a" stands for attitude, and the "t" signifies how an individual is treated. Consequently, if a person does not feel content in their environment, if the atmosphere fosters a negative mood, and if they harbour a negative attitude, then no matter their knowledge, experience, competence, or judgement skills, it all becomes irrelevant. If the environment fosters "functional", positive emotions that enhance an individual's operation, then the person's development and performance improve. This collaborative synergy often propels teams, institutions, and entire societies from one success to another, boosting resilience and making it easier to handle challenges. This situation underscores why inclusion is crucial and has now become a critical concept in business literature.

While individual attitudes and behaviours significantly influence performance, we must also consider the structural sources of conflict in traditional organizations. Often, the interactions between individuals, the structurally contradicting objectives and attitudes of the different departments and units they are in along with the functions they serve can lead to stressful environments and conflicts. However, this does not have to remain the status quo. The agile management approach, for instance, offers a solution for addressing these structural issues with its leadership philosophy, tools, methods, and frameworks. Agile management systems built on highly autonomous, self-managing teams which learn from their mistakes, where unnecessary hierarchy is minimized and decision-making is delegated to the lowest practical level, can indeed promise a very positive resolution in terms of attitudes and behaviours.

If we were to revisit the seed metaphor introduced at the beginning of the book, it can be said that an individual's performance is not solely determined by their personal capabilities and skill accumulation but also by how they interact with their environment and the effects of that interaction. Extending this to institutions, it is clear that there is a collective responsibility that falls upon the shoulders of those starting from upper management shaping the work culture to the executives who define the institution's human resources strategies and indeed to all employees. This might seem apparent so far, but the real challenge is how to effectively achieve it.

Are we beginning to look forward to the subsequent sections of the book yet?

Diversity and Inclusion

In one of his speeches, Şerif Kaynar, a prominent executive search professional at Korn Ferry, articulates the concept of diversity by suggesting: "If there are eight 70-year-old men on the board of directors of a company, I recommend adding a 25-year-old woman". This approach certainly checks the boxes for diversity. Indeed, diversity in organizations can be achieved through deliberate decisions and actions.

However, using this example as a starting point, one must ask, "Is that really enough?"

Consider this: what truly matters is how this "young female board member" would feel within the group, what the attitudes of the other board members would be, and how they would work together for every individual to achieve optimal performance in this newly established system.

Typically, diversity is seen merely as an action – deciding in which areas we need to integrate people who differ from one another. This leads to identifying specific characteristics and then finding and incorporating individuals who possess each characteristic into the team. While enhancing diversity is indeed an action, be it strategic or operational, leaving diversity unsupported by inclusion can lead to a scenario resembling disaster. Therefore, I would like to broaden the discussion on diversity from the standpoint of inclusion.

In the sections that follow, we will explore the concept of perspective diversity under the subheading of resilience. When discussing diversity, we are actually referring to the development of varied perspectives in varied situations, not just merely assigning labels to people. This is the functional approach. Conversely, diversity based solely on labels such as sexual preferences, belief systems, skin colour, race, minority status, and language only serves to deepen the divisions rather than unifying people. This type of labelling can reduce individuals to mere representatives of their respective categories, rather than recognizing them as complete persons.

The diversity and inclusion definitions of the EMCC Global Coaching and Mentoring Council[1] are as follows:

> *Diversity means recognizing the differences among us. Ethnic origin, gender, age, national origin, disability, sexual identity, education, experience, philosophy, political views, socio-economic background, religion, different thought processes and perspectives, and everything else considered to make us different can be included among these differences. Some of these differences are permanent and some may change and shift over time. Our differences are what makes us unique.*
>
> *Inclusion, then, refers to putting the concept and practice of diversity into action for individuals, teams, and work groups, organizations, and institutions. We all have a role to play. This means that we value our customers and colleagues without prejudice, respect them, support them, and appreciate the diversity they bring.*

Psychological Diversity

Inclusion can be seen as the external world's impact as reflected in our internal world, and the process of managing the emotions and thoughts brought on by these reflections effectively. In other words, each of us, due to a variety of factors, might find ourselves in a different place within our internal world, both physically and in terms of emotions and thoughts, even under the same external conditions. Perhaps the diversity created by our inner worlds is what is truly important. Just as each person's body may react differently to the same physical stress, so too might individuals respond differently, both psychologically and physiologically, to identical emotional stimuli. This diversity is invaluable for the resilience of systems; however, if the physical and emotional responses they provoke are not functional, they become detrimental.

Take the metaphor of the tree, for example. Let us allow each of our members to recognize where they perceive themselves concurrently. By employing the metaphor, we aim to raise awareness of what is needed and possible to bridge the gap between their current position and where they are or the position their organizations aspire for them to be. This approach essentially involves a "gap" analysis – setting goals, embracing them, evaluating the present scenario, exploring viable alternatives, and devising a plan for action from these alternatives – akin to a GROW methodology. I can recommend exploring some of the applications from www.blobtree.com.

Consider the image, and imagine it represents your workplace. Right now, today, if this tree were your work environment, where would you see yourself? Interestingly, your position might have been different yesterday and could

change again tomorrow. Where would you prefer to be right now? These are actually the same, fundamental questions: What is currently present, what is absent, and what would be beneficial if it existed? Where would you aspire to move? Harari suggests, "In the end, knowing yourself is what truly matters". It is vital to recognize what our inner selves are communicating to us.

This is not merely an individual exercise with a tree visual; all our team members are also positioned on various branches of this tree. Their specific locations are not the critical part. What is important is where they wish to be and whether they have achieved that position. Even if they are not where they desire to be yet, it is not that important. The key is being aware of it and recognizing how this positioning influences their interactions and reactions on that particular day, and to take the appropriate measures.

When considering inclusion, it is crucial to recognize that individuals might feel as though they are in a different place at any given moment. This does not mean they are permanently stuck and emotions ebb and flow. What is vital is the tree itself, encompassing all the roles within it.

For psychological diversity to be truly embraced, it is essential for an individual not to view someone different as a threat. We need to honour the anthropological and sociological reasons and aim to handle the psychological aspects within our inner worlds. Like all change management initiatives, this directs us towards engaging in dialogue with ourselves, listening to our inner voices, upholding our values, addressing our fears, practising self-compassion, adopting a growth mindset, and maintaining a non-judgemental dialogue.

Recognizing our differences as sources of richness, understanding that the patterns that have brought us to this point are more like prisons than protections in our evolving world, and accepting that change brings opportunities and is inevitable and that collaboration is much more effective when it occurs with people who are different from us, along with taking notice of the concerns, fears, and values we would like to protect which only serve to strengthen our resistance to change, will ensure that we embrace transformations much more comfortably. Moreover, in a rapidly changing world where we cannot predict tomorrow's threats, we need to face the fact that we cannot succeed, much less sustain our institutions by clinging to outdated structures and patterns, surrounded only by those who think, act, and live as we do. The solution lies within us. I promise that by starting with recognizing our own unconscious biases, understanding what we exclude along with the why and how of it, and then proceeding to expand our inclusion, the world we inhabit will become a far more liveable, easier-to-navigate place, even capable of providing greater abundance.

As individuals and as leaders of institutions wherein we fill the roles of decision-makers, I believe our most pressing priority is to forge an equipped, inclusive society resilient against digital transformation and climate threats. To achieve this, we must establish a societal order wherein individuals feel included and that their voices are heard, wherein they contribute to decision-making and execution processes and see that their contributions are valued. Once more, everything starts with the individual.

Diversity Fuelled by Our Backdrop Stories

Our experiences shape our perspectives. These experiences, which we have named as our backdrop stories, leave a kind of sediment that filters and assesses new experiences through a kind of metaphorical colour filter. Particularly if we have endured unresolved, painful, and significant experiences, numerous psychological mechanisms are activated that shape our viewpoints and, consequently, our initial reactions right from the start. This, of course, is excellent news for diversity. Only with such a rich and varied perspective can we fully understand the impact of an issue on all the stakeholders involved. In this context, diversity of viewpoints and perspectives is a tremendous asset and a significant advantage. However, if not managed carefully, these background stories can disrupt team harmony and make some individuals feel excluded, creating some very undesired outcomes.

Inclusion relates closely to diversity, equity, and equality. This is the feeling you experience in an environment where there is a sense of belonging, where it is reliable and safe, where you are respected, and where you feel your best. In short, it is your mood in the environment you are in. There are many factors that influence this, some of which are our backdrop stories.

There is a cartoon by Marco de Angelis called *Who Ordered the Apple?* where various fairy tale characters and real persons are depicted sitting around a big table where they are served one big red apple on a plate held by an apparently luxury restaurant waiter. So it is a dining table with a variety of individuals, each one of them representing characters who symbolize how the cultures shaped by our backdrop stories and what we have lived through in the background inevitably determine our interactions with any kind of new experience. We may encounter the same events, but our internal reactions may vary. Recognizing this phenomena and understanding our emotional triggers put us ahead. If not, we consistently remain in a passive state.

If you can have a look at that cartoon or any similar one with such a diversity of backdrop stories, let us consider the following questions. On the table:

- Which chair do you see yourself sitting in?
- What's brewing in your inner world?
- How does the conversation relate to your own story?
- Where are you on your personal journey at that moment?

The apple being served in this cartoon symbolizes any kind of novelty or change – be it a new manager, a strategic shift, entering new markets, launching new products, restructuring the organization, exploring new geographies, receiving a promotion, or changing job roles. These examples are just a few from the professional world. Personal life changes may include a new family member, welcoming a newborn, dealing with a daughter's new boyfriend, a new relative, moving to a new home, purchasing a new car, acquiring new furniture, meeting new neighbours, and so on.

It is evident that each change in our lives is connected to our past experiences. However, the critical question for inclusion is: how aware are we of the triggered emotions and thought patterns questioned due to these changes? If we are led to undergo change without acknowledging the stories of our past, without listening to them or understanding the emotions they evoke, we are more likely to feel excluded. Consequently, we are able to experience a very beneficial awareness by pausing, engaging in reflective practice, and listening to our inner voices. And what if I were to say that this approach should not be limited to ourselves but extended to every member of our team?

After all, when we understand how our backgrounds influence our journey towards inclusion, why not just extend this awareness to everyone we have an impact on?

Note

1. https://www.emccglobal.org/leadership-development/diversity

3

Leadership and Inclusion

I have been involved with the concept of leadership for many years. The subject of leadership, on which I have an academic interest, has been one of my focal points all throughout my banking career and in the roles I have assumed in civil society. This has remained the same as I have become a person whose writings, speeches, and opinions on the matter attract interest.

The importance of organizing human communities to work together harmoniously and achieve common goals is undeniable. However, the effective methods for achieving this have evolved over time and are currently undergoing significant transformations as well.

Our generation has witnessed cinematic heroes like *The Man Who Saved the World* (*Dünyayı Kurtaran Adam*) or *Superman* prevailing in movie theatres, and we grew up with history books which typically embraced the approach of presenting historical periods through the lens of individual figures. This dominant narrative of history and society focused on a central heroic leader whose actions shaped their community through their triumphs or failures, placing the entirety of responsibility on a single person. The leader also emerged as a hero, and a hero was someone who had suffered, made sacrifices, initiated change and transformation, overcome obstacles, and had defeated the enemies. This concept of leadership was widely accepted because the global perspective of the era was the same. History had always been narrated in this manner. However, paradigms of the past are not static. Today, we find ourselves transitioning away from this traditional view, especially due to technological and demographic shifts, although the approach remains prevalent in political life and geopolitical narratives. This shift has been the primary reason for me in writing this book.

Every concept comes with its counterpoints – dialectic, the Yin and the Yang. We see that the concept of inclusion, the underlying reasons of which we address from every angle and the recent importance of which we explain comprehensively in this book, has unfortunately not been able to halt the growing global polarization. In leading democracies, votes are nearly split down in the middle; politicians win by slim margins; and in many of the nations there is an increase in extremist views, populist rhetoric, and the impulse to forge common enemies.

Meanwhile, the dynamics of the business world and the technological and demographic changes affecting it particularly illustrate that societies rich in diversity supported by inclusion across all the dimensions outlined in this book achieve much greater success, prosperity, and peaceful cycles of life if they are able to preserve these qualities of inclusion and diversity. While I need not reiterate all the reasons here, I still want to highlight that even though we are still far from artificial intelligence becoming a reality, we are living in an era where machine learning has advanced very much and platform economies, largely governed by algorithms, have begun to shape numerous sectors and the dynamics of our lives. Therefore, it is quite clear that we must establish a societal and professional order that will irreversibly embrace diversity.

From this standpoint, I would like to briefly discuss the current understanding of leadership and some fundamental paradigms related to it.

Leadership Paradigms[1]

"You can take the horse to water, but you can't make them drink it"

Perhaps this is the saying which best summarizes the current understanding of leadership. In the initial years of our careers, many workplaces operated on strict directives. Everyone would perform their assigned tasks, those who excelled – and aligned well with company policies – would climb the corporate ladder, while others who fell short would eventually leave or would be let go. The course named "Management" during my university years was known as "Command and Control" in my mother's time. The primary goal was to manage and direct resources in the most effective way. The understanding of leadership was heavily intertwined with concepts borrowed from the military.

Almost everything has changed since then, but some companies still exert great effort to resist this change in organizational structure and style of management. Others adopt numerous cognitive methods to keep pace with the change, flattening hierarchies, establishing new structures, embracing agile management systems, and engaging in vision and mission workshops. They define corporate values and display them prominently on walls and websites. They try out nearly all there is, yet they often make little progress on the psychological dimension of the individual level. I guess this sentence may seem like a very bold statement, but I hope that within the entirety of this book, I had the chance to explain where the real issues lie and what the functional solutions would be.

Well, what is going wrong then? It can be said that in our societies, workplaces, or even our personal and professional lives, none of us wants to be coerced into agreement and be forcibly made to "drink the water". But assume that they have, effectively, "led us to the water". Then, there we may stand, never to drink.

One of the definitions I attribute to leadership in the current work environment is the *multilayer stakeholder network management*. We must manage our affairs not with instructions but by winning both the minds and hearts of each other. Everyone is a customer to someone else, and every department makes purchases from another. We must provide the best customer experience, in fact, to our own members. What happens if we do not? The recent trendy terms are "The Great Resignation" and "Quiet Quitting". Both of which point to a similar notion; that is, the effective leadership currently in effect is to make sure all stakeholders contribute voluntarily.

The critical concept here is the meaning we find in our jobs, the common goal which unites us in the workplace. As I often say, people are willing to endure hardship as long as they believe in the cause. Historical figures like Churchill promised "blood, toil, tears, and sweat" with success, and modern leaders such as Steve Jobs, Elon Musk, and Jeff Bezos have been able to attract top talent willing to work tirelessly despite their tough reputations. They do not seem to have employed any kind of soft, loving, warm, or embracing approach to leadership. So how did they manage to create such an allure? What made the people around them willingly "drink the water" and even guzzle it without the use of force?

Creating common value collaboratively with all the stakeholders, not through commands, coercion, or obligation but by winning hearts, is an expected characteristic in contemporary leaders.

"What does tomorrow's world expect from your leadership today?"

How can we, today, act as good "ancestors" for our future generations? What should we do differently?

When I start my speeches, I always ask: Please think of the people you value the most and list them in your mind. And now, please gaze upon our current experience here and go through the lens of these people in your list. Based on what you will learn here, what would be the best course of action that benefits the people you value?

If you or the institution you lead were to cease to exist today, what would humanity miss tomorrow?

What is that one unique thing the world expects from you?

We must stop navigating by looking in the rear-view mirror. How could dwelling on the problems of yesterday enrich the leadership of tomorrow?

What do you notice as a common theme in the sentences I have listed earlier?

We often focus on the leader – the leader's personality, character, charisma, energy, presence, proclaimed vision, actions, and ultimately, what they gain from their endeavours. This approach, unfortunately, positions us in a very narrow, constrained system. However, there are many factors that lend our existence meaning on this planet. When we shift our focus to these factors, ideals, and the people, our approach to leadership then proceeds to go through a transformation, gaining a profound and very powerful new meaning. Contemporary leadership is an approach which expects us to stop focusing on the leader or the institution as represented by the leader with all their stakeholders and start placing the legacy it will leave behind for future generations in the very centre.

Perhaps one of the worst things we do for our children is make too much of their birthdays. They are celebrated to such an excess that we end up embedding in their minds an idea along the lines of "You are the centre of the universe, the most unique among everybody and the one special above all others". It is nearly impossible for someone with this mindset to be truly happy nowadays, nor is it possible for them to make a lasting, positive impact on the systems they engage with. However, when we approach life with a curiosity about who and what our existence serves and what we mean for those we value the most, then, everything that takes place gains a new significance. When we pause to consider ourselves and the impact we have, we are able to obtain insights through a completely different lens.

By "what we value the most", I mean not only the people we care about but also other beings, nature, the universe, belief systems, spiritual dimensions, geography, ideas, and ideals as well.

So what does my life serve? And from the viewpoint of that which I serve, how should I aim to live it?

"Whose voice are we not hearing?"

Jeff Bezos made it famous; he added one extra chair than the number of attendees present, keeping the seat empty for the duration of the meeting.

The purpose of this empty chair was to remind us to consider the voices of those not present in the room, prompting leaders and teams which lead to continuously ask themselves:

- Who else is affected by our decisions and our action plans?
- Who are the stakeholders of ours not currently present in the room?
- Whose voice could render our decisions more inclusive if we hear it?

In recent years, the increasing complexity, rapid change, and uncertainty have demonstrated that the challenges we would not want to face the most can come from those stakeholders we overlook or ignore, not just from the stakeholders of the system we control.

Therefore, the effective and contemporary understanding of leadership should adopt an approach that seeks to constantly ask, "Whose voice can we further add to the conversation?" It is easy to overlook and ignore; the real challenge is to include the perspectives of those who are excluded.

"Corporate culture: what you begin to stop noticing three months after joining a new job"

The amount of importance we attach to creating a corporate culture is ridiculous. It is one of the most critical concepts for human resources teams, located at the very heart of their strategies. We know how important diversity is today, but still, we also keep striving to create a common corporate culture. Why is that?

It is because we know that managing a community with shared characteristics simplifies organizational efforts and reduces internal friction and conflicts, consequently minimizing discord within the system. It is a sort of engineering approach – like fish unaware of the water they swim in. Once employees are fully assimilated within the corporate culture, they become oblivious to the social structure they are embedded in. And what harm could there be in such a thing?

Some time ago, I gave a leadership training which resembled coaching to an audience made up entirely of the white-collar employees who worked in an institution that is cited as an example in the textbooks, a global leader among its sector and also the largest company of our country in its field. We had previously worked with hundreds of people before, and I noticed that the employees in this company only came from five universities. There was a place in this company for you, but only if you were a graduate from one of these five universities. And once you stepped in, you would encounter a tremendous company culture: training, directives, mentorship programs, sharing, opportunities provided to employees, values, and so on. Such an amazing environment.

So what is the problem with this incredible environment, you may ask. The issue lies in its insularity from the external world. The employees are unaware of the bubble they are in. Meanwhile, their customers and investors come from all walks of life. The result? As society changes, technology evolves, competitors shift, and new methods and applications potentially render some of their offerings obsolete; one day this company will be struggling to hire individuals capable of adapting to these changes. Because their ingrained culture is so overpowering, newcomers will often feel suffocated, alienated, and excluded.

Therefore, the contemporary leadership approach requires an understanding which recognizes the bubbles we live in, encompasses not just the internal but all of the stakeholders, and embraces differences without placing individuals in transparent social prisons.

That is why it is crucial to continually learn from the observations of new employees in their first three months. We need to constantly re-evaluate the corporate world we are shaping into existence with the insights these fresh perspectives provide.

"Partnerships are formed not by partners but by common goals"

How obvious, right? Yet it is a realization I have not come upon until hearing the sentence given earlier.

Previously, I have always considered the individuals in a business partnership as the pivotal elements, and similarly, I viewed marriage as just two people deciding to unite their lives. However, what truly mattered was the presence of shared goals and the combined future that would materialize when the individuals agreed to unite – not just side by side but together, crafting a monument to their convergence. This is situated not only on a cognitive dimension but also on the psychological one, involving the state of mind, the prevailing emotions, and the experiences born out of all these taking shape.

The recent trend towards *purpose-driven* companies underscores this principle with their underlying comprehension. Every institution exists for a reason. Then, what is this common goal that unites its stakeholders? To what do we serve by facilitating the emergence of this unity? What is the reason behind our choice in pursuing this collectively?

This notion is prevalent in political history, but it now extends to all forms of union, including corporate entities.

As a case study, you can watch a video I prepared on this topic.

In the video, I discuss the following: When Ben & Jerry's, a subsidiary of Unilever with an annual turnover of 2.2 billion dollars, announced a few years ago that they would not sell their products in the occupied Palestinian territories, the announcement caused a huge stir. Our focus was on what happened afterwards.

And you can similarly study the circumstances surrounding Disney's recent CEO replacement as well.

In terms of leadership paradigms, the real questions are about the shared goals and the collective purposes that unite us, as well as the emotions that envelop these endeavours.

Remember the adage: "Emotions unite people, while ideas divide".

"We do not expect the leader to know all the answers, just to know how to ask the right questions"

How could a single person know everything? In this incredibly complex and changing world, even if a leader is highly knowledgeable within the closed system they think themselves to be in control of, it is still impossible for them to be fully aware of the effects created by the constant shifts in external conditions.

For instance, who among us had experienced a pandemic before? Who had to manage the institutions they were responsible for, while the entire world was in quarantine?

There is a necessity for the leaders to become comfortable with uncertainty. The role of a leader is not to have all the answers but to pose the right questions within the right frames, fostering an environment where they collaborate with their stakeholders to create new perspectives and forge innovative solutions.

"Lead not the individuals, but the relationships between the members of the team"

In leadership practices, our focus now is not so much on the individuals that make up the team but rather on the relationships that form when those individuals come together.

Many leadership models are built on the leaders' individual, relational, visionary positions, and the competencies they possess. Models that centre on the leader are becoming insufficient in the face of the ever-changing life paradigms. In the past, leadership training centred on how to motivate team members and to prevent demotivation, along with creating common excitements, vision, emotions, and so on. Even situational leadership, a model I endorse in this book, primarily focuses on the situationally centred interactions between a leader and team members.

However, we now know today that the crucial aspect is not leading the individuals themselves but rather being able to lead the relationships among them. It is about identifying and addressing dysfunctions within these relationships, recognizing barriers and frictions, deciding how and in which way the members need to change and then proceeding to facilitate these changes.

What this means is that the contemporary understanding of leadership requires a shift away from you being at the centre, managing all your interactions with everyone, and to instead focus on discovering the dynamics of the relationships between team members and making them functional.

Unfortunately, much of the workplace friction is attributable to inert organizational and functional structures inherited from the last century. Why would conflicts arise between finance and sales, or logistics and production, when all these units aim to serve the same overall purpose? Is it not only possible for one of them to advance in their own field if they are all together at the same level? Yet somehow, the struggle keeps persisting among the learned helplessness inherited from the past.

Traditionally, management could create incredible systems, especially in the industrial sector, but the potential points of failure in the system would always be the people – necessitating stringent control measures. Namely what time they clocked in, what time they left, how much product they produced, how many breaks they took during the day, what screen was displayed on their computer monitors and for how many hours, the time they spent viewing which websites or the time they devoted to which computer application, whether they were out in the field and if so where, how many doors did they knock on, what they did during the time it took them to knock on two separate doors, what they ate, where they ate, with whom they ate, how much they spent for which item and even what was happening in their social lives along with the content they posted on their personal social media accounts, or in other words, a horrendous prison indeed.

This approach essentially needed to build such a prison to get the answers to its questions, all of which we can now very easily address to our pleasure with the use of the right technological tools. But if we do not shift away from this "prison" mindset, we inhibit the potential for individuals to exhibit their best selves and performance capabilities.

Thus, the focus is no longer solely on the leader or the individual team members to be led; instead, it is on guiding the relationships between the team. This is the reason why team coaching has become increasingly significant today.

"Success is not owned by the leader, nor the institution they lead; instead it is created collectively and by all the stakeholders within the system"

Success is often claimed by all but, truly, it is a collective creation of every stakeholder involved – and not the sole possession of any single entity.

The traditional "win-win" concept we were taught is now evolving; the Japanese have introduced the concept of "win-win-win", emphasizing that success benefits all involved parties and not just the immediate stakeholders.

Previously, the focus had been on the leader, and then it shifted to the team, as we have claimed that the success actually belonged to them. Yet now, it is acknowledged that success within a system is contributed by everyone involved.

If sales targets are met or exceeded, who is to thank? May there be a contribution from customers or even competitors?

To succeed not in spite of someone but to do so collectively.

Yet one must pay attention as this is not an argument against competition. Reflect on the poignant moment when the Japanese technical director respectfully bowed before spectators and opponents after a penalty shootout caused them to bid a heartbreaking farewell to the World Cup in Qatar – indeed, one of the most powerful moments to have been photographed.

"Ubuntu:
I am because of you,
And you are because of me"

We discuss a style of leadership that effectively mobilizes all stakeholders, not drivelling on about some Herculean figure carrying the entire weight of the world on their shoulders (like Atlas in Greek mythology).

In today's more innovative recent business models, a leadership approach with an attitude which involves an awareness on how to benefit from the competitor and the challenges that lie ahead is required. In this context, perhaps it is necessary to touch on the philosophy of Aikido. In Aikido, there is an art of transforming the energy of your opponent's move towards you, not by opposing that energy but by turning it into something that can benefit you in the most effective way possible. How would you transform a move coming towards you by using a bodily movement to benefit from it? Let us consider this metaphorically: instead of opposing it, how can you use the energy arising from all the movements coming against you to create success in everyday life?

Success is created by all the stakeholders in the system. Contemporary leaders must be able to approach the issue with this mindset and direct the emerging energy, along with new opportunities and possibilities, towards a common goal.

The Place of the Concept of Leadership in My Life

Throughout my education, I never really encountered a formal leadership training, and nor do I remember participating in any kind of leadership practice. Despite the lack of such a training, such leadership roles in my life start forming early.

For instance, I was class president for as long as I can remember. Was it because I was tall, performed well academically, or behaved respectfully? Or was it something unperceived linked to my family background? My character, the emotions that lunged me forward? Was it the impulses I experienced? I'm not really sure. My stint as class president continued until some misbehaviour during a study session in the second year of high school which resulted in me getting slapped the next day while everyone else got off with a reprimand. The principal had said, "And you are supposed to be the class president!" On that day, I stopped using the title, and unfortunately, I cannot recall who my successor was.

Nowadays, leadership is a hot topic everywhere. I was recently invited to talk about leadership at a middle school. Not sure of what to say, I faced an audience of youngsters equally unsure of what they expected to hear. This leadership mania is not just in schools; it also permeates universities with endless trainings and lectures.

My initial fascination with leadership was linked to public speaking. Those who have known me for as much as 40 years cannot believe it, but as a teenager, I was incredibly nervous about speaking in front of small groups comprised of even three people. Ironically, I had participated in poetry readings since primary school, though I never won any awards and do not remember speaking on behalf of the class at any ceremony. Perhaps I should ask my mother – everyone knows how bad my memory is. But after all, what is important is what I remember. Because our topic is not a short history lesson; it is about how these experiences shaped who I am today. In this context, my first significant exposure to public speaking was through the D.K.D. (Think, Speak, Listen seminars, a program based on D Carnegie methodologies), which were oratory lessons introduced to Türkiye by the late Nüvit Osmay. I had forced myself to attend these. While rhetoric is an aspect of leadership, it is not the aspect we are focusing on here. However, I think my early realization of the importance of addressing audiences and the momentum which I have gained through the exercises led me to introduce public speaking training and competitions to our country within the body of JCI Turkey during my thirties and to establish the ESU (English Speaking Union) institution in my forties, both of which have provided very valuable lessons on how younger generations could be equipped with oracy skills.

My personal journey with leadership truly began in 1996 when I became the president of JCI Istanbul and introduced leadership training to the organization, which proceeded to become known from thereon. Seeing a common thread in all the programs, I did some research and encountered the concept of NLP. I met in person with Anthony Robbins and attended his programs. All these sparked my interest in psychology, leading to my exploration of coaching and mentoring. This was complemented by reading and studying the works of authors like Daniel Pink and Malcolm Gladwell, attending related trainings and programs, and enriching what I had gained with even more materials over time.

However, there is a relevant saying I want to underline here: "Those who can, do; those who cannot, teach". Over 30 years in business and 25 in civil society, I have applied the concepts I teach both locally and globally in personal contexts and across institutions large and small. The lessons from my failures are many, but the successful methods and approaches I have developed comprise an even longer list. I must confess that over the years, the content of what I teach and discuss about leadership has evolved along with the changes in my environment, the needs of the world, and my own personal development.

What I am trying to convey to you here today is how I see the world. I discuss these topics to the extent that I believe they can be useful, drawing from historical contexts and personal experiences. However, I must also ask your permission for something. My stance on the things I have written in this book might change in the coming years as well. New experiences along my journey, the ever-evolving world, and the needs of the sectors and lifestyles I will be focusing on should eventually trigger such a change. So let us please consider the concept of leadership as something living.

Note

1. I'm grateful for various leaders I worked with for providing me inspiration for this chapter. I should highlight Ray Seamer, Peter Hawkings, Anthony Robbins, Kayra Akıalp, Andrew Buxton, Yavuz Canevi, Hasan Çolakoglu and Erol Sabancı.

4

Factors Affecting Our Capacity for Inclusion

Making Our Emotions Functional

As Brené Brown eloquently puts it: "Humans are not solely thinking creatures, they are rather feeling creatures who think occasionally". Despite this, both in the business world and in formal education, we heavily prioritize thought, often neglecting emotions. In professional settings, we have turned discussions on emotions into something which is frequently seen as taboo.

Leadership is essentially shaped by the contradictions we are able to manage. Sometimes we sabotage ourselves to avoid dealing with these contradictions or even prevent recognizing them. And in the other scenario, the emotions we are at peace with or those we are able to overcome define our spheres of inclusion.

Humans are inherently social beings, defined by their ability to interact with others. Throughout history, the existence of excommunication or solitary confinement as severe punishments highlight this fact, as they cut off a person's relations with others. Being social naturally involves emotions, and while humans experience a wide range of emotions, we rarely live with a conscious awareness of them.

Typically, when asked how we feel, our responses are general and superficial: "I'm fine", "I'm upset", "I'm angry", "I'm sad". However, our true emotional experiences are much more complex and nuanced. So why do we find ourselves stuck in basic emotional states like anger or happiness?

What does it truly mean to feel good or bad? Why do people struggle with emotional awareness? Psychologists believe it often stems from childhood, where some parents do not allow "permission to feel". You may ask, how so?

Many of us will recall hearing phrases such as "Boys don't cry" or "Boys aren't afraid". Similarly, girls will encounter stereotypical phrases such as "Don't get angry like a boy". These statements restrict and sometimes even prohibit emotions, causing all the unexperienced emotions to manifest through those that were permitted.

As a result, we either always experience emotions superficially or we do not truly experience them at all. This dynamic does not change much in the workplace. As there are families who view emotional expression as a weakness, often the existence of someone emotional can be viewed as a weakness in professional settings as well. But the truth is, if we are unaware of our own emotions or disconnected from them, we are equally unable to understand the emotions of others.

You may be wondering why it is beneficial to connect with our emotions. It is crucial because when we do connect with them, we are able to better understand our needs.

Emotional Analysis

Defining emotion holds incredible value. Performing an emotional analysis is a prerequisite to a fuller and healthier life. We should ask ourselves what we feel. Considering these questions is a good starting point for an emotionally driven understanding and for increasing emotional contact:

- What am I feeling?
- What makes me feel this way?
- What do I need as a leader?
- What does my co-worker need?
- What is happening right here, and in this moment, what is it that I'm currently experiencing?

- What do I want, and why? Or what stops me from wanting anything else?

A leader's ability to foster an inclusive culture hinges on their emotional alignment with the people they work with. Starting with acceptance and empathetic syncing are crucial.

If we, as leaders, hold the paradigm that "Expressing emotions is a weakness", then we must first change this mindset. For instance, rather than criticizing a colleague for trembling during a presentation by saying, "That's not how it's done. Your feet and hands are constantly shaking during presentations", we should open a dialogue that appreciates and congratulates their courage to express emotions and excitement publicly.

By doing so, we can convey that we see them, establishing a relationship based on understanding and recognition. Therefore, it can be said that the first step towards inclusion is to "accept" the emotions of our colleagues.

Just as important is to accept our own emotions as much as the emotions of those we work with. We must also recognize that our emotions can sometimes be misleading. In the end, it is our life perspectives which influence the accuracy of our emotions.

For example, if someone on the street does not acknowledge us, we might feel concerned, slighted, or angry. These are not "mistakes" or "improper feelings" on their own, but rather they are emotions about the accuracies of which we are uncertain. Consequently, after acceptance comes the step of reassessment regarding these emotions. For instance, we may ask, "Did I interpret this situation correctly?" Our communication should be clear and verifiable.

Another step is learning to regulate our emotions. Regardless of the circumstances, we can sometimes set our feelings aside and act rationally. For instance, it is not the anger itself that is problematic, but how we express that anger that can cause us problems.

Just like with everyone else, the inner child within us needs to be acknowledged and heard. Thus, we should listen to our inner voice but, at the same time, prevent it from impeding rational actions. There will always be a part of us that resists, and we need to approach this resistance with compassion.

We should treat our inner voice with the same compassion as if we were comforting a child with a soothing treat. Approaching our fearful, uncomfortable, or embarrassed selves with compassion and expressing that compassionate voice externally is what truly unlocks our potential to be an "inclusive leader".

Functions of Our Emotions

From the moment a person is born, they inherently possess certain fundamental emotions, and the rest are derived from these. There are theoretical differences within the field of psychology regarding the exact number of these basic emotions.

Let us adopt the simplest approach and consider that we have four.

Emotions are neither inherently positive nor negative; they exist because they serve a purpose. It is crucial to recognize our emotions in a way that allows them to be functional, to allow those emotions to be experienced where and how they should manifest. We need to recognize our emotions in a way that brings out this functionality because inclusion is about feeling good and safe; it is about the feeling that one belongs. We need to be aware of other emotional states that foster this feeling to be able to identify barriers to inclusion. If someone feels shame or is threatened, we cannot regard that environment as inclusive. We need to understand and address the reasons behind these feelings of being ashamed or threatened so that individuals can feel that they are in an inclusive environment.

Therefore, let us examine some of our emotions and assess their functionality.

Fear

The main reason we are born with the feeling of fear is due to our survival instinct. When we feel threatened, fear directs all our energy towards what we believe will save us at that moment. Fear is one of the most functional emotions and arises in the presence of a threat. Certainly, though, our perceptions of threats that trigger our feelings of fear have been subject to change over time.

So, as a leader, how should we approach someone who is afraid? What would be the function in this case?

Telling someone not to be afraid is ineffective. Instead, we should say, "I see that you're afraid, and I'm here for you". The best response to fear is to provide support and assurance.

Anger and Irritability

Anger is a very natural and human emotion. Although it is not as active as fear, it is close. Anger serves two very important functions:

- Protecting our boundaries
- Standing against injustice

So how do we approach someone who is angry?

The response should not be "Don't get angry", but rather, "I see that you're angry, and I want to understand why". The best response to anger is to allow the angry person to explain the reason for their anger. This allows the person to express the triggers of their anger, and together, you can discuss how to address them in the future.

Anger and irritability can also be expressions of some emotional states such as

- Loneliness
- Fear of rejection
- Depression
- Anxiety disorder
- Fear of being hurt
- Sadness
- Shame
- Humiliation
- Lack of support or help
- Jealousy
- Excessive stress
- Social isolation
- Chaos

Joy and Exuberance

These provide the energy to keep on living. If we encounter someone who is exuberant and joyful, it is necessary to share in that emotion.

Sadness

The function of sadness is to help us accept loss of any kind, and therefore, while being natural, it is a more passive emotion unlike joy, anger, or fear. The best support for someone feeling sad is to do nothing, giving the sad person space to experience their grief, and showing that you are there for them without rushing their recovery can be very beneficial.

In light of these, it can be said that the first correct approach for an inclusive leader dealing with the emotional states of their team members is to understand and accept the situation. Then, a roadmap can be drawn according to the needs of the person experiencing the emotion.

We must remember that all emotions are functional, but we need to know how to preserve their functionality. This can be achieved through the use of our inner voices.

Suppressing someone's emotional experience is not only harmful but dangerous. We must allow individuals the space to feel and express their emotions.

Often, we suppress emotions because we are unsure how to handle them. By saying things like "Don't be sad", "Don't cry", or "Don't be so happy", we inhibit the expressions of emotion. While this approach is functional for us, it certainly is not for the person feeling the emotion. Instead, we should consider why we feel compelled to suppress these emotions and what benefit, if any, this suppression offers us.

Emotional Intelligence

This is a good time to briefly mention emotional intelligence, which holds a very important place in human relations.

Emotional intelligence, which we refer to as EQ, consists of five factors:

- Awareness of your emotions (personal awareness)
- Management of emotions (will over emotions)
- Motivating oneself (using emotions in the service of a purpose)
- Understanding the emotions of others (empathetic dialogue)
- Management of relationships (social competence)

Emotional intelligence involves sharing the experiences and emotions of the person we are talking to in an open and reliable manner, or in other words, disclosing them, and it is extremely important for inclusive cultural development.

Sharing common values, experiences, expectations, and fears creates common bonds across differing points. However, excessive sharing can be overwhelming, such as when a person you have just sat next to on a bus, train, or plane starts telling you their entire life story.

Effective personal disclosure requires sharing information to the extent that it aims to establish trust and encourages the other party to be open in the relationship. To gain trust, you must trust as well. Before sharing personal details, ask yourself, "How will sharing this add value to the relationship?"

Personal disclosure can be done in three ways.

Empathetic Disclosure

Empathetic disclosure helps demonstrate (if needed) that there are, indeed, shared experiences or sentiments, which may be either real or perceived. Statements like "I was there too" or "I can imagine how annoying that is" are typical examples of this type of disclosure. In empathetic disclosure, it is often enough to show understanding or speak of the shared experience without delving into the details unless the other person expresses a desire to learn more.[1]

Manipulative Disclosure

This can occur in the form of two "close enemies", as it might appear similar to empathetic disclosure but serves a different purpose. Under the guise of empathy, manipulative disclosure aims to alter psychological dynamics between parties, potentially to dominate or influence the other person. Phrases like "It was worse for me" or "Not very believable, is it?" exemplify manipulative disclosure. In environments and relationships where inclusion is prioritized, such manipulative disclosure should be avoided entirely.

Emotional Disclosure

This type of disclosure involves sharing emotions that the other party may not be aware of and is a less common form of dialogue in business environments, but it can forge the deepest connections when used appropriately. But, of course, both parties need to be prepared, and the setting must be conducive to such openness.

In emotional disclosures, the effectiveness of your communication about your feelings and the emotional state you are in plays a crucial role. For instance, you might say, "I can feel the change you have experienced in your relationship with this person", or "I noticed a change in your enthusiasm when discussing this topic as compared to before. Last time, your excitement was so very palpable that it affected me as well. But today you seem disinterested. What's changed?"

Another example could be "I sense your hesitation when we discuss this matter" or "I can feel your commitment to achieve this goal", and you might also say, "I'm worried about the stress you seem to be under from your interactions with your manager. What if I were to say it might be mutual?"

Using emotional disclosure effectively can either support or challenge the dynamics of a relationship. It often requires bravery and, when done with awareness, can significantly deepen both the level of communication and relationships.

Empathy

Empathy stands as a cornerstone in fostering inclusion. It addresses one of our fundamental needs: not to feel isolated but to be seen, heard, and accepted just as we are. When we share our emotions and experiences, and what goes on in our inner worlds, we are not always seeking solutions or changes. More often, we simply want confirmation that we are not alone in our struggles. The goal of an empathetic conversation is not to fix someone or solve their problems but to share in the experience, affirming that we can endure together.

In the realm of inclusive human relations, the capacity to empathize emerges as perhaps the most crucial skill. However, it is often entangled with numerous other concepts, leading to confusion that hinders its appropriate application at times when it is most needed.

Empathy is a skill that must be cultivated actively. Humans are not born inherently empathetic; rather, we come into the world equipped with basic emotions and reflexes. Over time, as we navigate through life, our capacity for empathy evolves. However, it does not just naturally flourish – it requires intentional effort and nurturing. We develop our empathetic abilities by carefully and persistently engaging with our emotions and those of others, motivated by the diverse emotional responses and outcomes of our interactions and experiences. Empathy can be likened to an emotional and cognitive muscle that we possess.

Empathy is often described as "putting yourself in someone else's shoes" or "walking a mile in their shoes". However, these expressions can be misleading. The reality is that each person's life is profoundly unique, so no one shoe can fit another's feet. Even if the external circumstances are similar, our internal worlds would be different. Our perceptions of reality and psychological filters vary greatly.

We may feel the same way as another person at any given time, but our past experiences can never be truly identical. Those of us who have siblings can understand this better, as siblings raised in the same household with the same parents and having nearly led the same lives often develop into very distinct individuals, do they not? How, then, can we truly claim to put ourselves in another's place?

So How Should We Define Empathy?

Empathy can be seen as a practical application of compassion. If we do not want to feel, live, or be right there in the realm of the emotions, especially in the realm of pain caused by the circumstances in someone else's life, then how can we truly empathize?

Brené Brown says, "Compassion is a daily practice and empathy is a skill set that is one of the most powerful tools of compassion. The most effective approach with regards to meaningful connections combines compassion with a certain type of empathy, called cognitive empathy".

What does this mean, though?

"Compassion is about actively recognizing and accepting our shared human experiences, which allows us to extend loving kindness to ourselves and others. It's a virtuous response aimed at addressing the pain and needs of others through relational understanding and action". So compassion involves action – not merely "feeling" but "doing" as well.

Compassion acknowledges that every person's life includes struggles, and no one is exempt from pain. Hence, in compassion, there can be no thoughts of superiority like "I am better than you" or any impulses such as "I can heal you and fix your problems".

As the American Buddhist nun Pema Chödrön writes in her book *The Places That Scare You:*[2]

When we practice generating compassion, we can expect to experience our fear of pain. Compassion practice is daring. It involves learning to relax and allow ourselves to move gently toward what scares us . . . In cultivating compassion, we draw from the wholeness of our experience – our suffering, our empathy, as well as our cruelty and terror. It has to be this way. Compassion is not a relationship between the healer and the wounded. It's a relationship between equals. Only when we know our own darkness well can we be present with the darkness of others. Compassion becomes real when we recognize our shared humanity.

Close Enemies of Empathy

It is quite straightforward to discern the opposite of any concept. Thus, identifying situations devoid of empathy, as we have discussed so far, should not pose a significant challenge. Let us consider this:

Imagine someone who lacks empathy. How would you describe them?

Take a moment to list five characteristics.

Also, recall at least three instances where you have observed these traits.

Maybe consider a scene from a TV show, a play, or a literary work that exemplifies a lack of empathy?

We could even go further: Let us write a scenario or craft a story featuring characters who are devoid of this feeling – an antithesis of empathy.

See? It seems unnecessary for me to reiterate what an empathy-deficient individual looks like here. You have already written it down in the most beautiful and effective manner possible.

However, the true peril lies elsewhere. The greatest challenge for inclusion stems from phenomena perceived as empathy but which actually sabotage the sense of inclusion.

These are wrong actions taken with the best intentions, grounded in past patterns, genuinely believed to embody empathy – or worse, they are the insidious approaches we know to yield negative outcomes yet proceed with them anyway to fulfil other emotional needs under the guise of appearing empathetic.

Let us examine these deceptions. Termed "close enemies of empathy", these behaviours closely mimic empathy to such an extent that they appear identical, yet they are in fact the most insidious enemies and the most damaging saboteurs of it. So what are these phenomena?

Sympathy "Poor thing, what has befallen you? Oh dear . . ."

Sympathy, which might seem like empathy's greatest ally, is perhaps its most insidious foe. Alongside antipathy – also a constant companion – sympathy is fundamentally a human emotion. Perhaps these are reflexes we have developed anthropologically to survive, cope with hardships, and protect ourselves from threats. Sympathy enables us to suffer together and suffer in the same way, also serving as a reminder that we may also face similar difficulties. It alleviates our loneliness, even if it is through a reflection from someone else, and reminds us that we are alive. Therefore, both sympathy and antipathy, innate from birth, are profoundly useful to us.

Empathy and sympathy relate to how we respond to someone else's emotional experiences. Sympathy involves adopting the other person's feelings and sharing them, which can be physically and spiritually draining. Empathy, however, focuses more on understanding these feelings rather than sharing them; it involves both connection and distinction.

When we are sympathetic, we might like to say, "I'm so sorry for you". In the process of empathy, however, this phrase transforms into "I understand, I feel the same. I too have been/am there in my own way, within my own reality". The key distinction between them lies in the situational positions they express. In a sense, the emotional distance between two people always differs. One might feel, "Such things would not happen to me or to people like me", or, "I hope it doesn't happen to me and my loved ones". Conversely, while saying, "Oh dear, poor you", we do not truly meet the other person where they are; instead, we place them in a position we ourselves wish to avoid, perhaps as a way to emotionally shield ourselves.

The problem? Whether consciously or not, the other person senses that they are, in fact, far away from us. Instead of feeling included, they feel excluded. How can one express pity and simultaneously stand beside someone in solidarity?

A *Judgemental Attitude* "Oh no, that shouldn't happen. You should do this or that in such a situation".

When we listen to someone's story and if a judgemental voice arises within us, we may actually feel ashamed for the person speaking. For example, if you are listening to someone's harrowing experience and suddenly find yourself gasping at how terrible the situation is, then the person being judged cannot experience a feeling of inclusion. Of course, it is nearly impossible to stop judging because throughout our lives, we have developed many thought patterns to simplify the complexities of life and make them more understandable to us. These patterns intervene in such a scenario. For example, if a person who believes in the "If you work, you win" mindset observes the disappointment of someone who has lost without working or making an effort, and then thinks, "You didn't even do anything, how can you come to me and speak of your sorrow?", then the inclusion is interrupted once again. Yet perhaps the person conveying the issue thought that they had done the right thing according to their own patterns. In such a situation, instead of two people talking, the embedded thought patterns within them start to converse, and as they judge each other more and more, they begin to exclude one another. The way to turn this into empathy is to allow that voice inside us to speak, even if it expresses a reflection of our own world, and then to focus again on the feelings and thoughts of the person in front of us. Being with them, where they stand, does not necessarily mean we approve of them. Indeed, if the person in front of us expects this, then it means that their expectations lie beyond the realm of empathy.

Disappointment   "Oh, what have you done?"

How can someone who feels they have disappointed someone else with what they have lived through feel included? They will want to see you as a dependable, just individual who will collaboratively address the issue with equity. Yet what they will perceive is a depiction where each revelation of theirs results in disappointment. True inclusion cannot thrive under such conditions. How can you expect help from someone who is disappointed by your flaws?

Blame   "Terrible, who could do such a thing? I wonder who the real culprit is".

Since shame is instinctual and contagious, we can feel it on behalf of others. It is the situation where one is faced with an embarrassing turn of events, and rather than adopting an empathetic stance, their immediate reaction is venting their discomfort and vulnerability through blaming and scolding. This is commonly seen in parental reactions when a child shares an embarrassing story. For instance, parents might react by asking, "Who did this? Let's go complain, beat them up, or punish them". Take the example of the parents who try to comfort a child who has hit their head on some furniture by saying, "I'll beat the couch". These children grow up with the reflex that they can escape their situation by blaming someone else. And, of course, there is a parallel blame involved as well, along with it comes a hidden accusation: "How could you allow this to happen?"

Consequently, there are no witch hunts in empathetic conversations. The goal of an empathetic conversation is not to achieve a shared relief by locating the guilty party. Because finding the guilty and attributing the fault to them is a passive stance, the situation moves away from a process which grants the benefit of letting us recognize the emotions we have suppressed and the feelings we have covered up or what we could do differently from now on and how we might be able to feel in the future.

Avoidance "It couldn't have happened like that . . ."

When we cannot face difficult emotions, or when we prefer to keep them at bay, our tendency is to minimize and evade them. With phrases like "No way, you're exaggerating", we might actually be refusing to accept the emotions, pain, or suffering of the person we are listening to because of our own discomfort. We might utter, "It's not that bad". There may even be such a strong reflex to avoid the situation that we end up forming sentences like "You are actually amazing, perfect. Look, everyone loves you". What just happened here? The subject matter drifted away from us; we have avoided it. But now, the person across from us is left alone with their feelings. While we think we are helping by listening to them with our utmost humane feelings and by speaking the words we believe to be beneficial, in reality, we have distanced ourselves by covering up not only the emotions we avoid but also the person experiencing them as well.

Comparison   "That's nothing, listen to this . . ."

Instead of connecting through shared experiences with the person in front of us, we may fall into the urge to assert superiority by comparing their situation with others. Phrases like "What you've experienced is nothing compared to what I've been through" are examples of such behaviour. Our sentences may not be as striking as the one in this example, but still, every time we compare what the person in front of us tells us with other experiences, we are actually excluding them instead of including.

This phenomenon is quite common. Rather than engaging in a true dialogue, it often feels like two parallel monologues. One person might think, "I don't care what happened to you; right now, my situation is what matters. Why are we even talking about you?" This thought should be the one that surfaces when someone suddenly realizes they are merely a bystander in the other's narrative while discussing their own issues. In such scenarios, it is unclear who should include whom. Both parties might seem to be engaged in an empathetic conversation, yet they slowly drift apart. This occurs because, instead of focusing on one person's emotional state and mood, two distinct emotional states start to clash, bringing the empathetic dialogue to an end.

Disbelief   "You couldn't have done or experienced that".

When you hold the person next to you accountable for expressions, interpretations, or behaviours that disturb others or cause conflict, this reflex can kick in. Rather than adopting an empathetic stance like "That must be hard" or "You are very brave", accusatory remarks such as "I can't believe you said that to them!", "You shouldn't have gone there", or "You can't talk to people like that" begin to surface, precluding any inclusive dialogue.

Of course, two similar situations emerge here. When the listener really does not believe what is being narrated, the conversation moves away from being a "close enemy" and turns into a conversation that is clearly not empathetic, and everyone immediately recognizes this shift. However, more insidiously, while continuing to engage as though they believe the speaker, someone might utter, "I don't believe it" merely as a pattern of speech. This introduces a cognitive dissonance, as one might think, "If you believe, let's talk; if not, what am I doing here?", thereby ending the empathetic conversation. But of course, we refrain from articulating such things and continue to convince ourselves that we are being empathetic, while internally the conversation we are having just serves to exhaust and even sadden us deeply to the extent that we become martyrs to it.

Solving the Problem "I'll handle it for you".

When we see a difficulty or pain, we might feel an urge to fix the situation. Indeed, societal order has probably developed such a reflex within us. If someone presents a problem, there is an expectation for a solution. We will either solve it or give advice on how it can be solved. But starting to solve it rather than listening and empathizing shifts the interaction from empathetic engagement to a problem-solving dialogue.[3]

Believing that we can solve someone else's problem is very far from empathy. Instead of being in a place where we understand the situation, feelings, and the reality of the person in front of us, assuming a stance of "I know better than you, I can even solve your problem" distances us far away from being empathetic. Even though the problem might be solved in this way, it does little to address the emotional experience of the situation.

Empathetic Dialogue

When considering inclusion in empathetic dialogues, our aim is to empower the person experiencing tough emotions to better cope. However, often we neglect this emotional dimension and inadvertently sabotage the process as we have explained earlier.

How, then, can we develop tactical suggestions for fostering more effective empathy?

Consider these questions, and how they might prove beneficial regarding the matter at hand:

1. What can we do to be mindful of the strong emotions of the person we are conversing with? How can we observe the dominant emotions? These emotions might sometimes be hidden, but body posture, tone of voice, and other auditory/visual cues give them away.
2. How can we show sufficient understanding to thoroughly comprehend the emotions and perspective of the person we are engaging with and how much time can we dedicate to this?
3. How can we control our own perceptions regarding the emotions and perceptions of the person we are talking to? Statements like "You seem quite angry about this" or "I thought this topic would worry you" are some examples of such a situation taking place.
4. How can we truly accept the emotions or perceptions of the person from their point of view?

5. If we find ourselves invalidating the legitimacy of the person's emotions, how can we shift our approach? What needs to change for us to be able to say, "It's very normal to feel angry about this"?
6. How can we initiate a supportive kind of dialogue in our conversations with others? Proposals such as "Shall we work together for a solution?" might be of help.

Compassion and Empathy: Understanding the Difference

The difference between compassion and empathy might be challenging for us to fully understand, which could constitute a significant barrier in our process of developing our capacity for empathy.

Compassion and empathy have now become terms we have started discussing in the business world as well. For example, a study in the United States found that approximately 20% of companies ensure that their managers receive empathy training. According to the same study, the best skills for successful leadership were found to be listening and responding.

Of course, as a recent and even somewhat popular concept of our day, namely the "Burnout Syndrome", becomes more prevalent due to modern work challenges, the focus on compassion and empathy as probable responses has intensified, though often, differences in the definitions of these concepts have begun to blur.

So what is compassion? What is the definition of compassion? How is compassion different from empathy? I see these terms being used interchangeably in many places. But this is not correct.

Empathy and compassion stem from the same desire: to better relate to and understand the experiences of others. While both are beneficial for personal and organizational health, they play distinct roles in daily interactions, and there are differences between someone who is empathetic and one who has compassion. Understanding these differences and consciously choosing your approach is very important with regards to leadership. It can be the determinant of whether you and your team members feel functional emotions or not. Research suggests that focusing on compassion and mental health fosters strong, sustainable leadership and enhances self-awareness.

Let us explore what compassion is and how it differs from empathy. Additionally, let us address why it is important to show both compassion and empathy in our lives.

"Wisdom without compassion is ruthlessness, compassion without wisdom is folly".

Fred Kofman

What Is Compassion?

According to *Psychology Today*, "Compassion is an empathetic understanding that is accompanied by a desire to act on behalf or sacrifice for a person". Simply put, compassion arises when you care about someone's situation and want to help them. You see someone in a troublesome situation and you want to go where they are. For instance, you might encounter someone who has dropped their shopping cart and proceeded to help them pick up their groceries. Each small action throughout the day can balance some of the more difficult emotions.

Additionally, the concept of compassion suggests putting yourself in someone else's shoes, differentiating it from mere "kindness". Kindness can be pragmatic and devoid of empathy for another's suffering. However, there often is an overlap.

Compassion is kindness that stems from appreciating other people as real individuals who also suffer. Giving up your seat to a pregnant woman, being polite to retail workers, helping a friend move – compassion can take many forms. Paying it forward with positive actions throughout a day can do anything from bringing a smile to someone's face to even preventing burnout.

As long as it is motivated by genuine care, almost any act can be compassionate; the ultimate aim should be to alleviate suffering.

Compassion and Empathy: What Is the Difference?

Definition of empathy: Empathy is our awareness of other people's feelings and our attempt to understand how they feel.

Definition of compassion: Compassion is an emotional response to either empathy or sympathy which creates a desire to help.

So what makes compassion different? Unlike empathy, compassion creates an emotional distance from the individual and the situation. By practising compassion, we can become more flexible and improve our overall well-being. Bloom says, "Careful reasoning mixed with a more distant compassion [. . .] makes the world a better place". Compassion creates an emotional distance from the individual and the situation we face. We often allow other people's feelings to affect us, even misjudging them based on our own prejudices. But I believe we have the power to prevent this.

Empathy is an understanding of our shared humanity, and actually, it is deeply rooted within ourselves. It awakens the desire within us to understand the feelings of others. This primitive, instinctual urge is what psychologists refer to as cognitive empathy. There are numerous reasons to cultivate empathy, not only because it benefits our personal health but also because it enhances our professional relationships.

However, what psychologists describe as emotional empathy presents a challenge – it is the other side of the coin. Emotional empathy extends beyond mere understanding; it involves a deep, sometimes overwhelming desire to experience the pain of others.

Research highlights that our empathetic intentions, while noble, are not without bias. As we try to be empathetic, we unconsciously become more sympathetic to individuals with whom we form close relationships. Such a situation diminishes our ability to connect with people whose experiences do not reflect our own, as empathy results from a feeling of "sameness". Being human can provide a good starting point, but beyond that, it is impossible to escape our biases.

Power and How We Use Our Own

In Cartesian thought or within an engineering approach, we define power as the extent to which one can overcome the resistance against them. But it does not always have to be defined this way. Power is also something described as harmony. In Taoist philosophy, a leaf flowing in a river is in its most powerful state because it carries all the river's power with it – underscoring the position of being a catalyst, facilitating, and channelling power rather than possessing it.

When we look at it this way, the concept of power moves away from the idea of crushing resistance and forcibly imposing actions upon other systems and individuals. When considered alongside harmonious living, it begins to benefit all the stakeholders within the system we are part of.

There exists a concept which is spoken of often: "win-win". But did you know that the Japanese always say "win-win-win" instead? In this way, they remind us that we need to find solutions where not just both sides win, but all stakeholders do so. A system is never made up of only two parts. There are many other stakeholders that make up that system, who may not be sitting at the table in that moment, who may not be in the room, who do not appear on the balance sheet, and even those whose voices are not heard. When we consider the concept of power, we must also include all other stakeholders that we do not notice, whom we overlook and ignore at that time.

From this perspective, when our approach to power is fed by a non-judgemental stance, it becomes even more functional. Not opposing the person or concept before us, but instead fully understanding, respecting, and comprehensively addressing the issue at hand makes us much stronger.

To avoid resisting or blocking with the intent to shatter the energy of those in our path or the challenges we may face, and to abstain from adopting a passive or a victim-like stance against overwhelming odds. Just like in Aikido, comprehending the power coming towards us, aligning it with ourselves, using it as leverage, and incorporating its strength into ours to achieve desired outcomes. Now, how does that sound?

We can ask ourselves these questions:

- How can I channel the events that befall me to create something functional?
- Rather than resisting power, how can I leverage it to create something effective?
- In my current environment, in order to facilitate the most functional outcome, how can I transform the oppositional forces to work in my favour and create effective results?

Rather than imposing something on other people, excluding them, or using our privileges to reach a priority position in the system we live in, we should instead focus on the subject of how we can achieve better, more functional and beneficial results.

Power, not manipulative and at the expense of others' interests, is about what we can create together in the society we are in. We must consider, while you and I might benefit, what can we also create to ensure that those whose voices are typically unheard also gain?

When our approach to power and philosophy in life are like this, all the concepts we touch on here will support an inclusive stance. Adopting any other approach will result in us creating resistance against inclusion and then trying to crush said resistance. It is when we define power this way that it gains a meaning with inclusion. But otherwise, it unfortunately turns into a contradictory force.

Trusting and Feeling Safe

Trust is increasingly seen as an essential element in human relationships. Just as a car's engine quickly becomes unusable without motor oil due to friction, relationships devoid of trust inevitably deteriorate.

So how do we develop trust towards someone or an institution? Simply hearing "Trust me" is not enough. Have you ever felt an immediate, strong sense of trust just because someone told you to trust them?

Viewers will surely remember the television series titled *24*.[4] In the series, whenever law enforcement officers, government officials, secret agents, and even police officers said, "You can trust me", "We are taking you to a safe place", or "You are safe with us", both the series's heroes and we, the viewers, would feel the presence of a likely threat. Trust is not built merely through assurances. Then it is beneficial to look at what the feeling of trust is and where it comes from.

Charles Feltman, in his book titled *The Thin Book of Trust: An Essential Primer for Building Trust as Work*,[5] defines trust as "[b]eing able to risk something you value by leaving it unprotected against another person's actions". This implies leaving something valuable – whether it is a person, a thing, a concept, or a work – completely unprotected and vulnerable, risking it against the actions of another person, system, or entity that could have an impact on it.

Suppose you have a small child or a baby, and you and your spouse are going out to dinner in the evening, so you call a babysitter to your house. You entrust your baby to this person and leave.

Imagine you have spent days and months working on and creating an architectural project model, and you need to take it to a presentation, but your flight gets delayed and you do not have time to pick it up from the office and head to the client's location. You call a colleague from the office and say, "Pull a taxi off the road, put the model in the back seat, give the taxi driver the address. I will be waiting for them at the entrance of the building".

Consider these other common scenarios requiring trust: Moving into a newly constructed building in an earthquake zone, sharing a secret that no one should know, lending money, buying art from NFT markets, going on a trip, extending your hand for a handshake, or even saying "Good morning" to some person. Think about most of the things we do during the day. When do we perform these acts without any internal alarms going off, and when does caution kick in?

Would not it be something if the concept of trust could be distilled into a formula? After a STEM-based education, followed by an engineering education, and finally becoming a banker, I constantly feel the need to find such formulae. Of course, fitting abstract concepts into a formula is not always correct and possible. But if we cannot define, we cannot observe, and what we cannot observe, we cannot measure.

We cannot significantly enhance our understanding of a concept without measurements. However, it is important to remember that our goal is to continue on this journey of development. When we encounter a new concept, we must define it, observe it, and develop our abilities related to it. But that is not all; we also need to know when, where, and how to apply these skills, thus bolstering our reasoning capabilities.

Is merely building reasoning skills sufficient? Not quite. We must also foster the desire to utilize the appropriate skills at the optimal times and places. This means that we need the following:

- Competence
- Reasoning
- Motivation

If we address and develop each of these separately, then we can talk about increasing our capacity on a subject. So how will we define and increase our capacity of trust? Let us try to define the concept of **trust** first:

In her book *Dare to Lead*,[6] Brené Brown talks about **BRAVING**, a formula which she designed after decades of work. The name is an acronym made up of the initial letters of the following words:

B (Boundaries): For trust to develop, it is essential to establish clear boundaries, which can be thought of as a set of rules encompassing guidelines and actions. If it is not clearly established who is responsible for what actions and where these actions are to take place, we are likely starting off in an unhealthy situation.

R (Reliability): Okay, we are positioned to meet certain expectations. But can we achieve the same level of performance consistently? Will they follow through on their commitments? When faced with conflicting expectations and rules, can we still count on them to consistently fulfil our expectations?

A (Accountability): Will they take responsibility if the expected performance is not achieved? Moreover, will they assume responsibility if a loss occurs? Will they remain present during unpleasant situations and share in the consequences with us?

V (Vault): Who will share what information with whom? Will my privacy be respected? Will they share information about me or our shared situation with others? What should remain confidential, and what can be disclosed? Will they use what they know in a way that could harm me?

I (Integrity): Will they stay true to the ethical framework that united us? Will they betray the principles and values we share? In difficult situations, will they compromise these important principles for situational solutions?

N (Non-judgement): Can I interact with them in complete transparency without being labelled or pigeonholed? Can they assess me and the situation without judgement, accepting me as I am? Naturally, I would feel disinclined to stand alongside a person who judges me from various other angles, apart from the common subject which unites us.

G (Generosity): Will they interpret any action, word, and intention in the most positive way and be especially generous emotionally in their attitudes and behaviours towards me?

I am not sure how this came across to you when I outlined these one under another, but if you would like, you can evaluate each, one by one and with an example.

For instance, consider the babysitter you hired to care for your baby at home. First, have you clearly agreed upon expectations? When discussing "babysitting" do all parties have a consistent understanding of what that entails? Establishing trust becomes significantly easier if all parties have a clear and mutual agreement on everything from the broadest concepts to the finest details in advance.

Years ago, when I lived in London, our daughter was still a baby. With no family support nearby, leaving her for just a few hours in the evening to spend time with my spouse became a very significant challenge. I think we had about half a dozen babysitters, each from a different country. That is when I witnessed the cultural dimension of babysitting. For example, most of the babysitters from the day care and those who came to the house were undressing our daughter completely as they were putting her to sleep. We, on the other hand, were dressing her in several layers of pyjamas and covering her before sleep for warmth and comfort. The child was confused, to say the least. Our expectation was that the babysitter would engage with her, wear her out with play as it were, and help her settle down to sleep by the time we returned, so we could both enjoy our evening spent outside and be happy about the subsequent night of restful sleep. Later, we realized that the easiest way to babysit was to put the baby to sleep and watch TV. Every time we came home and ten minutes after the babysitter took their money and left, our daughter woke up energetic and seeking our attention, having already had her nap. That was when we realized that a restful night of sleep was but a distant dream.

In addition to agreeing on all the details, consistently meeting expectations is another topic of importance. We have all witnessed how Turkish wines have improved in recent years. Despite all the economic difficulties, tax burdens, and so on, our wine producers have made remarkable progress. But if you ask, "Is every bottle of wine the same quality?" I still cannot comfortably say "Yes". As a result, when purchasing my favourite wines, I find myself buying extra bottles to account for potential variability. The prices are already quite high, and when I consider the likelihood of encountering a bottle that does not meet expectations, I find myself thinking, "Should I switch to imported wines with a standard quality?"

Taking responsibility is a critical element in building trust. What would happen if things were to take a wrong turn? Consider this scenario: you have paid substantial premiums to an insurance company, but they refuse to cover your damages after an accident, citing a previously undisclosed clause. Would you trust that company again?

Privacy and confidentiality form the foundation of any trusting relationship. We once had a house cleaner who did an exceptional job. She was strong and fast, often finishing early enough to enjoy a coffee break with us. It was during these breaks that we were forced into learning about all manner of things we should not know about. She would go on and on about the state of everyone's house, of the neighbours we knew or did not know, delving into their private lives as well. The woman was like a walking encyclopaedia. Eventually, after one or two instances, we reached a point where we would leave the house with an excuse just as she was about to take a break – whether it was shopping, picking up the child from school, or something else that urgently needed attention. Creating an excuse felt better than being subjected to the stories. Naturally, this made us wonder what she might be sharing about us elsewhere. Over time, we noticed that we had started tidying up the house before she came, even cleaning it a bit so that others would not hear about how untidy, messy, and disorganized we were. Needless to say, we could not maintain this relationship for long.

Honesty often depends on the context – it is a situational concept tied to an ethical framework. What is considered right in one situation may not be right in another. The vital element is that the transparency and adherence to principles we expect from each other remain consistent.

Another crucial aspect of building trust is ensuring that judgement is withheld. People tend to constantly judge each other; it is a natural human tendency to categorize others as either friend or foe. To do this, it continuously adds labels to everyone it communicates with. Knowing that a situational topic I mentioned will come back to me as a fixed trait label is a very challenging notion.

In the early days of my career, I was in a customer-focused position. Of course, this required attending dining meetings with customers. I was quite young at the time, and I was very excited about my experiences, so much so that I did not hesitate to share them. A few months later, when I heard someone refer to me as "*wining dining* Rıza" during a credit committee meeting, I was shocked. In the end, all I have done for our bank, the results that we have achieved, the sleepless nights of commuting, the Saturday mornings where I have shown up to work; none of these were even taken into account, and with that, I was labelled. As you can imagine, my circle of sharing customer-related experiences became very, very small after that. I hardly shared my experiences with anyone else because I was now afraid of being judged and labelled.

Have you considered the role generosity plays in building trust? We often hesitate to share a positive word, feeling, or compliment. Even when someone is generous in this regard, we immediately doubt what is behind it. Yet how appropriate would it be to start interpreting everything positively in a relationship founded on trust?

Over the years, there is an exercise I have conducted more than a hundred times in my training sessions: I split the participants into twos and line them up so that they face each other, where every person standing is only one foot away from their partner. First, one row, then the other, they all step forward at the same time and whisper a nice thought they have observed, perceived, or felt about the person opposite to their ear, and then go back to where they stood before. The process repeats, rotating the line so that each participant hears a positive remark from half of the group and makes their own remarks in return. Invariably, every group initially struggles with this exercise, but as they open up, how the energy in the room becomes palpable is something to be experienced. Interestingly, it is hard for some people and even some cultures to say nice words, while for others, it is hard to hear them. Isn't it strange? Our perspective is so focused on the negative that a nice word turns our entire inner world upside down. It feels incredibly good, but for some reason we deprive everyone around us of this gift and, naturally, ourselves as well.

How did this discussion resonate with you? How is the issue of trust shaping up for you now? We are not establishing a formula here; there are no determinations being made about how many units of trust there are, nor are we plotting a trust index on some graph, but hopefully, this discussion was still able to provide you with a good starting point.

You may find the use of the **BRAVING** formula to be enlightening when you review your relationships and determine what went wrong at which point in time. It might clarify the points where your system is losing trust and make such situations easier to understand.

Could we extend this formula in terms of **inclusion** to community trust? Is the trust within a community merely the sum of individual trust levels? Perhaps, in addition to trust among individuals, we might consider the community as an entity in and of itself and evaluate our trust in it using the same criteria. Can institutional trust be broken down in a similar manner? And if so, what should the decision-makers in the business world pay attention to? The trust that stakeholders have in each other and the trust each one has in their institutions are both extremely important, even by themselves. Each individual, while preserving their diversity and serving it, will expect this trust to be established in order for them to contribute positively to the organization and to express their original, genuine selves.

You might want to re-watch the series *Ted Lasso*[7] with this perspective in mind. It contains excellent examples of how a team coach, acting as a catalyst, fosters trust among all stakeholders. Though I probably should not be the one to praise this series, as it has won almost every award imaginable.

Of course, we cannot simply overlook the concept of self-confidence. As Brené Brown suggests, the **BRAVING** principles can be applied to self-confidence issues as well. I agree. Consider using the approach to discuss self-confidence issues with yourself or your inner voice. Address each question in the formula to your own self.

Let us see how the results turn out.

Instead of Pressure, Psychological Safety

Jürgen Klopp, a world-renowned and highly successful soccer coach, is a figure who comes to mind when the issues of psychological safety arises. He portrayed one such example of psychological safety and inclusive leadership to soccer fans and indeed to all of us with a striking example through Tyler Morton, who, at the age of 19, joined the Liverpool team as the latest academy player. During an interview about his debut, Morton was asked about his recent experience of playing for the first time in front of over 50,000 passionate fans, to play with a superstar team that had recently won the Premier League and the Champions League.

As most would agree, it would actually be a moment full of stress and pressure, not just for someone who is 19 years old but for each and every one of us. Who knows what was going through his mind when he was in that atmosphere of the match, stepping onto the field for the first time in front of fifty thousand fans and millions of others watching him in front of their screens. According to Morton, just as he started walking towards the field, Klopp turned to him and said, "The responsibility for playing well or badly is not yours, it's mine, because I chose for you to play. So your part is just to play freely and enjoy the moment". How about that? How often has someone created such a space for you in your life?

In that anxious and stressful moment, Klopp decided to instil confidence in his player by alleviating the pressure. This prompts the question: under what conditions can you create a similarly safe space and for whom? How would one be able to approach any differently to an enthusiastic, well-intentioned player? Clearly, adding more pressure would have been counterproductive. Therefore, Klopp's approach has served as a profound example of inclusive leadership, leaving a lasting impression.

What are some of the barriers which prevent this type of leadership from being more widely demonstrated? What is it that holds us back?

Your team probably aspires to excel at their tasks. No one enjoys underperforming. However, to enable your team to operate freely and without fear, it is essential to establish a sense of psychological safety. This means finding ways to reduce the pressure rather than exacerbate it, allowing team members to engage in their work naturally.

The concept of psychological safety, along with fostering an *inclusive* organizational culture, is becoming increasingly vital. If you are looking to quickly establish psychological safety within your team, there are some key strategies to consider which would afterwards be able to facilitate such an environment.

Unconscious Biases

We are all subject to conditioning through a numerous amount of factors. I lived through such an experience as well. I was the representative of a French bank in Türkiye. We did our jobs well. Our office was modest, and besides me were only two long-time colleagues and my driver. My colleagues only asked for freedom and autonomy, and they performed exceptionally well. Whatever I asked of them, they got it done. They were able to work anytime they liked and from the place of their choice. I was not one to visit the office very often. However, during the first few years, I occasionally found myself wondering during the day: Where would they be now? What would they be doing? Although everything was going just fine, the impulse to control was ingrained within my mind. This was because, up until that point, I had always been the one under scrutiny. I used to report my every move: where I was, what I did, my comings and goings, with whom I met – everything was monitored. I had worked under such management and also within such institutional cultures. I knew intellectually that granting people freedom was the right approach. Yet there was always a voice inside me, questioning. Eventually, I managed to shed this trait and was able to relax. But the process took years.

In summary, we are driven by numerous emotions and impulses that shape us into who we are and guide us to the places we currently inhabit. While these feelings and impulses have forged our identities, they are also able to manifest themselves as barriers.

Consider which of your traits that have brought you success until now might serve to hinder your progress moving forward. You may be thinking there is nothing beyond this point. But if so, consider this: some of your traits might be increasing your costs in the life you are leading. For example, my musings on where my colleagues might be cost me some precious moments of happiness. Within those moments when my mind wandered to my team, I was in a mental place where I should not have been. If I were to call or make any inquiries, I would be disrupting their work and inadvertently be sending a message that I did not trust them. And I did trust them, which makes for quite the paradox. So what patterns or habits might be contradictory to what we have outlined above?

As such, the greatest barrier to our success often lies in our unconscious biases. From the moment we are born, various norms, ideas, and even emotional patterns gradually wrap around us, moulding our personalities and social identities. Each one, in a way, constitutes formats imposed upon us by our families, our society, and in the contemporary world, even by social media. These factors are deemed necessary and often beneficial for fostering a more harmonious or homogeneous society, creating more compliant individuals, and maintaining a more predictable and controllable societal order. However, as Marshall Goldsmith's book title suggests, "*What Got You Here Won't Get You There*". The new challenges posed by the VUCA environment, contemporary management approaches like agile methods, and technologies such as remote collaboration, augmented reality, cognitive competencies, and data analysis methods are pushing us to organize, manage, and achieve results in ways that enable productive collaboration among individuals from vastly different disciplines and from all walks of life. It is within this context that inclusive leadership has started to become something indispensable.

Project Implicit: Unconscious Associations

"There is an 'I' within me"

So how can we take notice of these conscious and unconscious biases?

Have you heard of an initiative called Project Implicit?[8]

In my leadership training over the years, I have consistently posed the question: Who is the most important leader in your life? This query, as an introduction with regard to group dynamics, has consistently proven to be invaluable for our work. Participants would share with the larger group whoever they thought was the most important leader in their lives. We would then go through most of them, one by one, focusing on the qualities that made these leaders so important to the participants who mentioned their names. The recurring answers, influenced by the varying priorities of the group, typically highlighted names like "Atatürk", "my father", or "a senior family member", and occasionally, "the president of the football club I support". Ultimately, the objective was to lead participants to recognize, after a lengthy process of sharing, that they are indeed the most significant leaders in their own lives – a crucial realization for the training programme's goals.

However, over the years, my perspective shifted as I delved deeper into unconscious biases and the connections we form without realizing. I recognized that the "me" which we often refer to as ourselves wasn't a phenomenon as straightforward or comprehensible as one might think.

Consider the phrase, "I don't feel like it". Who is the "I" in this context? It would be no problem if it were me. But something within me does not feel like it. It is paradoxical because part of me wants something, yet there is another part resisting it. What a headache. This dilemma highlights a complexity that emerges just as participants grasp that they are the most crucial leaders in their lives and graduate. How nice. Bestow awareness to people in that they are the most important leaders within their own lives, and then fail to answer the question of, "What is this inner 'I' inside of me?"

In psychology, there is a concept known as "conditioning" or "priming". Our brains develop numerous "short circuits" and "thought pathways" throughout our lives, shaped by the patterns of our families, close circles, and those of trusted figures who have both knowingly and unknowingly taught these patterns to us. Because otherwise, constant re-evaluation of every situation with all its details, reassessing every moment of life and each one of our relationships repeatedly in light of every unique condition, and then activating our decision mechanisms with all of their capabilities would effectively make our lives unbearable. Thus, our brains optimize this process by linking specific reference points in the most efficient manner and making the basic, and even automatic, instinctual decisions with a great speed, continuing the process. This might be one of the most crucial protective mechanisms evolution has given us, so that we are able to maintain our sanity through such a complex life cycle.

Yet our brains are a hub of chemical interactions as well. Still, as somewhat of a burgeoning expert in the field of *neuroscience*, I'm not here to lecture you. Instead, I'll share this concept using the simple terms I employ with my four-year-old daughter, as maybe this approach would be much more suitable for the purposes of this book. Of course, I'm sure many of you know this subject better than I do, and that there are those who will read these lines and then proceed to learn much more about it. Science is progressing very rapidly in this field. So, if you find it appropriate too, let me summarize the topic here as I perceive it, but please, if you find any significant errors, details that need correction, or know of any (reasonably sized) new information that needs to be added, do reach out to me. We will be able to correct it in new editions and update it in the online resources prepared for the book. As I said, our purpose here is not to dictate facts in a field humanity has only just begun to explore, and is in the process of constantly re-evaluating its discoveries, but to create an understanding of how our brains' activities affect our daily lives with the limited amount of information at our disposal. We focus on how we can act or think differently to enhance our functionality.

I would also like to share a memory about neuroscience: In January 2019, I was in Kuala Lumpur for the launch conference of the EMCC Asia Pacific Region. Let me quickly add a couple of impressions here: It was my first time visiting a real Hindu temple in Kuala Lumpur, and it was also my first authentic experience so closely connected to the Indian culture. I felt how much the human population has grown as well, feeling it as I navigated the crowded public transport, the streets, and the squares. I experienced a new dimension of globalization, evident in the prevalence of Netflix screens at every corner. Previously, our visual cues for globalization were McDonald's signs, but now we have adapted to diverse cultural food preferences. Currently, it is the time of impulses which directly target our brains. Anyway, at the opening conference, there was also a quite elderly British scientist continuing his work in the Far East, who had been one of the speakers. When you speak about a topic unknown to the audience, an insatiable curiosity and appetite develop in the hall, and the speaker derives great pleasure from this. As I have experienced it many times, I am quite familiar with it. It is not a healthy situation at all, but as a speaker, it can even turn into a temptation that might lead one astray. In such a moment, the speaker was giving his lecture accompanied by MRI images of the human brain, and the topic shifted towards the differences between the male and female brains. Out of my personal respect for the speaker and because the etiquette of a host would not allow heckling (as I was the global president of the hosting organization), I listened to the scientist without interrupting his speech, but once he finished, I could not hold back and immediately went over to him, and in a private moment, I said, "These things you are showing, these differently coloured MRI images of male and female brains, do they constitute a cause or a consequence?" He could not answer and did not seem much interested in answering either. Thereon, the conversation turned a bit argumentative. "If", I said, "this is a consequence, then what we're seeing is how men and women in societal life develop different aspects of their brains based on the roles and responsibilities assigned to them, and if that is indeed the case, then we stand to gain many insights into how each individual might develop different aspects of the brains they possess. But if what you said was that these two brains are inherently very different, which had been the atmosphere created in the hall, followed by all the jokes, clichés, and so on, then you've pushed us towards such a conclusion without any attempts to elaborate. And if we don't possess concrete scientific evidence in the direction of what this suggests, then you have just done something terrible. In that this approach has destroyed the possibility of a harmonious society, free and inclusive in quality, and one that depends on individual choices". He responded even more harshly to my harsh critique, but I pressed on, saying, "With this approach, if we had examined these images a century ago, one might have argued that the brains of black individuals or Asians were fundamentally different from those of Western white individuals. This perspective is deeply flawed". Fortunately, after this exchange, he recognized the potential direction of our conversation, and the tone shifted towards a more genuine dialogue. He confessed, "When I first started my career as a psychiatrist in England, we were sent to prisons to 'treat' homosexual prisoners. At that time, homosexuality was viewed as a disease that needed curing". On one hand, here are the continuous discoveries of new tools and daily advancements in science through technology, and on the other, we still grapple with evolving social structures, patterns, and approaches. Change is constant but not unidirectional. Often, it is one step forward and one step back, and what constitutes progress for some may seem like regression to others. This underscores the notion that what got us "here" will not get us "there". What we accept as right today might soon be deemed incorrect very quickly and vice versa.

In my training sessions, I ask participants to close their eyes, raise their arms, and point a finger upwards, and wait for my command. When this exercise is conducted in a large hall or with the seats arranged in a circle for a clearer view of the people to see each other, the experience is enriched even further. With everyone's eyes closed and fingers pointing skyward, I instruct, "Without opening your eyes, please turn your arm so your finger points north. No opening your eyes". Naturally, it is a surprising request, and although most participants are unsure of the direction, they make a choice and adjust their arms accordingly. Following this, I tell them, "Now, please open your eyes but keep your arms still, and look around the room". Typically, they observe arms pointing in various directions, which inevitably leads to laughter. To this scene, I add, "Everyone's north is their own . . ." prompting even more laughter.

Of course, we then lower our arms, take our seats, and start a group discussion about the exercise. Some participants, either equipped with a physical compass or in recent years those with compass apps on their smartphones, and those with a keen sense of direction, often interject, "Professor, north is actually over there". However, as the discussion progresses, it becomes clear that the primary focus of the exercise was not about finding the true north at all. They soon realize they have been referring to the magnetic north. In the Mediterranean basin, this distinction may seem trivial, but as you travel farther north, it becomes evident that the geographical North Pole and the magnetic north differ significantly – by approximately 2,000 kilometres. I do not wish to digress too much, but it is interesting to note that there are actually three different North Poles discussed in navigation, and the magnetic pole shifts about 200 kilometres each year.[9]

So what does this all mean? If even our so-called scientific facts have such variance in definitions and approaches, almost everything we consider true becomes merely a pattern of belief that shifts over time with new discoveries. Consider the example of homosexuality, which, in many parts of the world, is no longer viewed as a disease. The truths of yesterday – the doctrines and beliefs people once died for – are changing rapidly, making way for new patterns of belief. During a discussion on this topic, a participant once shared, "Professor, I think I understand what you're getting at. My father-in-law was told by his doctor to avoid eggs due to high cholesterol. For years, my mother-in-law wouldn't let him eat them, although he loved them. It was always a topic of contention. But now, they say eggs are fine, and his doctor has given him the green light. So he missed out on his favourite breakfasts for years for no reason".

Stories like these illustrate our point. We devise the best solutions, ideas, and life strategies based on the information we have at the time. However, it is crucial to remember that what is accepted as truth today might be disproven tomorrow. This evolution of understanding is inevitable. The real tragedy lies in clinging to the outdated truths of yesterday, fighting against an ever-changing world with a deep sense of betrayal. Nonetheless, constantly shifting our beliefs and thoughts with every new piece of information could lead to even more chaotic outcomes. I believe the art of living well hinges on how effectively we adapt to change.

Avoiding Unconscious Biases and Connections: 10 Tips

After much discussion, it might seem like we have strayed from our main point. Fortunately, the earlier text provides a reference. Now, let us focus on how our brains function concerning these unconscious biases and unnoticed connections. From what I understand, our brains work within an energy structure, where energy flows through channels among structures known as nodes, continuously processing thousands of sensory inputs.

Our unconscious biases present one of the most significant challenges to inclusion and the kind of leadership needed today. So what actions can we take to mitigate these biases?

Whether they be conscious or unconscious, here are some of the things we can do to reduce their likelihood of emerging:

Awareness   The first step in combating the negative effects of our biases is to acknowledge their existence. Recognizing that there are factors which can alter our perception of events increases the likelihood that we will exercise caution when forming judgements or making decisions.

Evaluating the Current Factors Influencing Our Decisions It is crucial to question whether there might be factors causing you to over-trust your beliefs or overlook certain information. Be wary of falling prey to the bandwagon effect or adopting a stance merely because it is the popular choice.

Reflective Practice Approach for Reviewing the Past Identify patterns in how you have previously perceived situations and pinpoint where you might have erred. For instance, if you consistently overlook facts or rely too heavily on intuition, this is an area for growth. Take the time to approach opportunities for further discovery of the data available to you.

Curiosity: Benefits and Focus Curiosity can be an adept tool in combating cognitive biases. It encourages us to pause long enough to ask questions, which can prevent us from hastily assuming we are correct.

Internalizing a Growth Mindset People with a growth mindset believe that cognitive abilities can be developed and are inclined to learn from criticism. Instead of covering up mistakes, they see them as opportunities for learning.

The notion that some factors are "fixed" or immutable is a misconception. Cognitive biases can be modified through concerted effort and practice. A growth mindset is just one of many heuristic methods that can steer you in the right direction.

Identifying Current Anxieties   Consider what or whom might be misleading you at this moment. Reflect on what triggers your responses and whether a bias might be influencing your perspective.

Challenging Your Initial Reactions   Try to understand issues from multiple angles to enhance your critical thinking skills and view the world with more empathy. Challenge yourself to consider the opposite of your initial reactions and explore the outcomes.

Seeking Diverse Perspectives   Actively seek feedback and different viewpoints from others. Their insights can help you identify potential blind spots and combat overconfidence.

Evaluating Unverified Assumptions   Go out of your way to seek information that contradicts your current beliefs.

Intellectual Humility   Intellectual humility is about remaining open to the possibility that you might be wrong. This approach involves questioning your convictions rather than staunchly standing behind them.

We all have cognitive biases, but there are proactive steps we can take to reduce their negative impacts on our decisions. Doing so can help improve our relationships and enable us to make better decisions.

Cognitive Dissonance

In this section, we delve into cognitive dissonance and its underlying theory. We will also examine the triggers and impacts of cognitive dissonance, differentiate it from cognitive biases, and, more importantly, discuss strategies for reducing cognitive dissonance.

We often define ourselves by traits such as honesty, diligence, and health consciousness. Yet there are times when our actions do not align with these self-perceptions.

This inconsistency, known as cognitive dissonance, can be profoundly unsettling. Many of us seek ways to escape this discomfort, often without realizing that it can lead us to behave or feel in ways that seem out of character. By understanding what cognitive dissonance is, grasping its powerful influence, and learning methods to manage it, we can be able to take steps towards regaining control.

What Is Cognitive Dissonance?

Cognitive dissonance can be defined as the psychological tension felt from trying to reconcile two or more conflicting pieces of information. Typically, to resolve this tension, we either adapt our beliefs to form a new coherent understanding or dismiss the contradictory information.

Unlike hypocrisy, which is always the first thing to come to mind when discussing cognitive dissonance, it poses a very personal risk – threatening our self-concepts and identities. Throughout our lives, we tend to believe we make decisions based on objective information and experienced events.

We also tend to think of our brains as small but potent supercomputers, and we fantasize that they process facts and produce rational decisions.

However, reality is somewhat more complex.

While we think we are receiving information objectively, what happens is, actually, the opposite. Several cognitive biases can alter our decision-making process, potentially leading us to make poor decisions and act irrationally.

In 1956, psychologist Jack Brehm observed a phenomenon where individuals, when given a choice between two similar options, tend to perceive the option they chose as superior. This observation has come to be known as the "free choice paradigm" in psychological literature. People will even begin to enumerate the advantages of their chosen option, regardless of how similar it actually is to the alternative.

To explain this phenomenon, psychologist Leon Festinger introduced the concept of cognitive dissonance. He proposed that individuals were driven to reduce inconsistencies within their own self-perception in order to maintain their sense of identity. This hypothesis has become a foundational concept in social psychology, explaining why cognitive dissonance occurs and how we react to it.

Causes of Cognitive Dissonance

Cognitive dissonance typically arises from a discrepancy between what we believe and how we behave. Festinger's theory highlights three primary situations as the triggers for cognitive dissonance: forced compliance, decision-making, and effort.

Forced Compliance

When individuals are coerced into actions that contradict their beliefs, it naturally results in discomfort. To alleviate this discomfort, they often concoct justifications for doing this unacceptable thing to make the situation seem more tolerable than it is.

In a laboratory experiment on cognitive dissonance in the 1950s, participants were asked to perform a monotonous task for an hour. Afterwards, as they left the experiment venue, they encountered individuals who were not privy to the nature of the task. These unsuspecting individuals were approached by different groups of participants who were incentivized differently to convince them that the task was enjoyable: One group was paid $1, another $20, and a final group was not compensated at all.

Surprisingly, it was the group that was paid just $1 who later reported enjoying the task the most.

What changed their attitude if the task was inherently dull? The crux lies in the brain's need for cognitive consistency. Since the task was not justified with a sufficient monetary reward, they developed an internal motivation to justify the lie.

Decision-Making

When we make a choice, regardless of its magnitude – from what to eat for lunch to deciding on a place to live – we inevitably reject an alternative. This decision-making process can be stressful, especially when both options seem equally appealing or unappealing. To ease this psychological discomfort, we often rationalize our decisions through a process known as "spreading of alternatives".

Suppose you have the option to go out with friends or stay home for the evening. You had fully planned to go out, but it starts raining. You think to yourself, "Maybe I should stay home. It'll save me some money, and I can always see them another time".

You inform your friends of your decision to stay home, but they push back, reminding you, "We've already bought your ticket. You have to come!" Reluctantly, you agree, reasoning, "I don't want to upset them or waste the ticket. Plus, getting out might be good since I've been cooped up at my desk all week".

This rationalization constitutes your attempt to reduce dissonance. When you can align your behaviours with your values, you feel better. Initially, staying home seemed appealing because it aligned with your desire to save money. However, deciding to go out became justifiable when afterward you considered values of health and relationships.

Effort

Humans inherently value outcomes that demand significant time, effort, or resources. We often equate cost with quality under the assumption that "you get what you pay for".

When an effort does not immediately appear "worth it", we instinctively find reasons to justify why it surpasses other options. Once we have invested time and energy, which cannot be reclaimed, we convince ourselves of indirect benefits to make the expenditure seem worthwhile.

Take, for example, starting a new exercise routine. You join a gym and opt for a premium membership with a personal trainer. A few months into your routine, during a dinner with a friend, you proudly discuss your progress and assert that the money was well spent. Your friend, surprised by the cost, interjects.

"Really? You paid that much? You could have gotten the same package for half the price at my gym".

Faced with this revelation, you cannot undo your workouts, nor can you get a refund simply because there was a cheaper option available. So you do the next best thing. Instead of feeling bad about your hasty (and expensive) choice, you quickly list all the positives: you rave about your trainer, the convenience of the gym's location, the discount you received for paying upfront, and speculate that you might not have been as committed had you paid less.

This process of justifying the effort helps you maintain a positive outlook on your decision. You want to continue feeling good about it, so you stack the reasons in its favour.

Effects of Cognitive Dissonance

When faced with cognitive dissonance, we generally respond in one of three ways: we change our behaviours, adjust our beliefs, or rationalize our circumstances to make sense of the discrepancies.

By far, the healthiest intervention for dissonance is taking consonant action. For instance, although we recognize that reducing screen time is good for us, many of us still spend extensive hours in front of computers every day. To reduce this internal conflict, we could decrease screen time, take regular breaks to rest our eyes, or use blue light filtering glasses.

However, when we do not take action, we often downplay the significance of the conflicting information. "Well, my job requires a lot of computer time", we might say. "There's not much I can do about it. Anyway, this website (which would be one of many) said it's probably okay, so I won't start to worry".

Persistently living in a way that contradicts our values can profoundly affect our mental health and psychological well-being. We start to feel disappointed, ashamed, and defensive about our behaviours. Our values act like a set of coordinates, guiding us to be at peace with our decisions. When our actions do not align with these guides, we may find that the lives we live do not reflect our desires.

Signs of Cognitive Dissonance

At their essence, cognitive biases are mental shortcuts designed by our brain to process information more efficiently and make faster decisions. They serve as mental shortcuts to help speed up our information processing.

They help us understand and decide faster. In this manner, they are regarded as "adaptive tools".

These mental shortcuts exist to make our brain more efficient, but they can create systematic errors in our thinking as well. This happens because they rely not on actual facts but on our perceptions, observations, and experiences.

In reality, we see the world through our filters and make decisions accordingly. Recognizing that these filters are not "real", but that they rather reflect our unique perceptions and experiences is crucial.

Cognitive biases may cause us to ignore unpleasant information, overlook important facts, or even perceive non-existent patterns.

Although most of the cognitive biases we experience operate unconsciously, we can still take steps to avoid them. Before moving on to how we can avoid cognitive biases, we must first understand the biases and identify the situations where they most frequently emerge.

There are no obvious warning signs that indicate the instances when our actions do not align with our values, leading to internal dissonance. Some of the signs that we are compensating for such a mismatch include the following:

- Defending our choices more than seems necessary
- Avoiding certain conversations or topics
- Feeling angry, irritable, or anxious without a clear reason
- Experiencing envy or resentment towards others' successes, feeling compelled to explain why it is not happening for us
- Justifying our actions extensively, even when unchallenged. Devoting unnecessarily excessive amounts of energy and time to this endeavour.
- Surprising those who know us well with our explanations or behaviours
- Insisting to others that our perspective is the corrected one
- Downplaying the potential dangers or unhealthy outcomes of our behaviours
- Feeling uneasy discussing personal matters or when talking with those who disagree.
- Reacting in a hostile manner to even mild, constructive, or perceived criticism.

Cognitive Dissonance Versus Cognitive Bias

Cognitive dissonance and cognitive bias are related, but they are different from one another. Cognitive dissonance occurs when there is a contradiction between our thoughts and actions, leading to psychological discomfort or stress because our behaviours are not aligned with our beliefs.

On the other hand, cognitive bias is the tendency to process information through the lens of our experiences. Our brains rely on patterns, past experiences, and mental shortcuts in order to process information quickly. When we receive new information, we do not interpret it objectively; rather, we see it through the filter of our existing beliefs.

Cognitive dissonance can influence our cognitive biases and vice versa. Typically, when we feel psychological discomfort, it is because one of our thought patterns is being challenged. We may then develop these biases to avoid discomfort or to change our behaviours.

Social psychologists have identified dozens of cognitive biases, some examples of which would be the confirmation bias, the fundamental attribution error, or the sunk cost fallacy.

Common Types and Examples of Cognitive Bias

Amos Tversky and Daniel Kahneman pioneered the study of cognitive biases in 1972, showing that people often make irrational judgements and decisions.

Today, there are dozens of studies in social psychology and behavioural economics which serve to validate various cognitive biases.

These examples of cognitive bias usually stem from ignoring relevant information or overemphasizing an inconsequential but salient feature of a situation.

Let us look at some of the more common biases that have drawn the most attention from researchers and those that have the most significant impact on how we navigate the world:

Confirmation Bias: This self-serving bias leads us to seek and prioritize information that supports our existing beliefs while dismissing information that contradicts them.

For example, if we only consume news from sources that align with our political or economic views, we are likely to experience confirmation bias.

Anchoring Bias: This bias describes our tendency to rely too heavily on the first piece of information we receive, even though subsequent information might contradict these early facts.

An example of anchoring could be when we see a house priced at 1 million lira and then perceive another house priced at 500 thousand lira as cheap. However, if the first house we had seen was priced at 200 thousand lira, then the house which costs 500 thousand lira would have seemed expensive.

Ingroup Bias: This bias leads us to favour and trust people within our social group while not extending this goodwill to outsiders.

For instance, discovering a shared favourite sports team or alma mater with someone might automatically endear them to us, making us assume they are a "good person" due to this connection.

Fundamental Attribution Error: Also known as the actor-observer bias, this bias involves believing that our actions are due to situational factors, while others' actions are due to their fixed character traits.

For example, if someone cuts us off in traffic, we might think they are inherently rude or a bad driver. However, if we are the ones who cut someone off, we attribute it to being late or reacting to someone else's driving. This constitutes an example of attribution error from our perspective.

Hindsight Bias: This bias involves seeing events as more predictable after they have happened.

When people see the outcome of a decision, examples of hindsight bias occur. This might be a business decision, a political election, or even an underdog winning the basketball game. People will feel as if they "knew it was going to happen all along".

Halo Effect: This bias occurs when our impressions of others in one area influence our overall impressions of them.

If a beloved celebrity is accused of a crime, the Halo Effect may lead us to dismiss the news as false because we love this person too much to believe it is true.

Self-Serving Bias: This describes our tendency to attribute our successes to our own efforts and our failures to external factors.

For example, a student might credit their intelligence and hard work for good test scores but blames an unfair teacher if they receive poor grades.

Sunk Cost Fallacy: This logical fallacy describes our tendency to continue a behavior because of previously invested resources. An example of one such related saying might be "to cut one's losses".

Have you ever felt obligated to finish a meal because it was expensive? Or continued to invest money in repairing a car because you had already spent a lot on it? Then you may have experienced the Sunk Cost Fallacy.

Negativity Bias: This bias is the idea that something we perceive as negative will have a more substantial effect on us compared to a neutral or positive event.

We give more weight to negative outcomes, some of which could relate to negative feelings, social interactions, or events.

Attentional Bias: This bias describes how a person's perception can be affected by what they are currently focusing on.

We might experience this when we buy a new car and suddenly start to see the same model everywhere. Yet, in reality, nothing has actually changed.

Overconfidence Bias: Some types of biases can manifest as personality traits.

You may have met someone who thinks they can do everything. This is overconfidence bias.

It involves an inflated perception of one's abilities, intelligence, or skills. In some scenarios, this quite dangerous bias could lead to disastrous outcomes. We might overestimate our driving skills on the highway or our knowledge of the stock market.

This bias is closely related to the Optimism Bias, which makes us think that we are less likely to experience negative events.

Why We Should Try to Eliminate Biased Thinking

There are several reasons why we should strive to eliminate cognitive biases and biased thinking.

At its core, biased thinking complicates our ability to engage in proper information exchange. We avoid information we do not like, and we may fail to recognize information that could lead to a more accurate outcome. Biases impair our critical thinking and can lead to irrational decisions. Finally, they are likely to harm our relationships. Biases can cause us to make incorrect judgements about others and then act based on those judgements.

Ways to Reduce Cognitive Dissonance

Although your brain naturally attempts to resolve cognitive dissonance, this does not mean that you cannot actively participate in managing the process. Here are four steps to recognize psychological discomfort and cope with it:

What Emotions Do You Feel, and Where Do They Manifest in Your Body? Cognitive dissonance often triggers a tangible physical sensation. Whenever you experience physical or psychological discomfort, take a moment to note it. You do not need to address it immediately – instead, consider reflecting on it later in a journal or discussion.

Imagine this scenario: You commit to drinking eight glasses of water daily, but during a lunch outing, you choose a soda instead. A friend playfully teases, "Haven't you reached your water quota today?" You notice a mild tension in your stomach. Although it is clear they are jesting, you feel slightly irritated.

What Would Happen If You Chose Not to Avoid This Discomfort? Instead of getting defensive, consider what your reaction is telling you. Ask yourself: What was your first instinct when you felt this emotion? What triggered my emotional response, and when did it occur? By identifying the cause of your discomfort, you can address it more effectively.

In the given example, you felt uncomfortable when your friend teased you about choosing soda over water, as it highlighted a discrepancy between your stated goal and your actions.

What Needs to Change? Now, you are at a crossroads. You said you would do one thing but did another. Here are several ways in which you could resolve this:

- You could call your friend and tell them to never speak with you again.
- You might justify your soda choice by noting that it contains water, so it is basically the same thing.
- You could continue on Google until you find a website that says nobody needs to drink eight glasses of water and that water is actually unhealthy.
- Or, alternatively, you could accept the slip-up and commit to your water-drinking goal moving forward.

The crucial part is not the choice itself but the awareness it brings. At this point, you have already done the hard work. Recognizing and questioning the dissonance are usually enough to resolve it.

Cognitive dissonance is not a punitive force; it does not compel you to choose one path over another. It provides valuable information that can help you feel at peace with your decisions and understand why you make them.

How Coaching Can Facilitate Change The adjustment described above might seem simple, right? However, sometimes the root of dissonance is not immediately clear or is more complex. In such cases, or when significant behavioural changes are necessary, seeking external support can be advantageous. Talking with a coach can enhance your self-awareness and help you identify the origins of your cognitive dissonance. Coaching is a practice that guides people through stages of behavioural change and helps alleviate internal discomfort.

These kinds of inconsistencies are part of the process that makes us who we are. Even when we want to change them, we find it beneficial to approach these inconsistencies with curiosity and grace.

Cognitive dissonance is an essential tool for building self-awareness. We need these mechanisms to recognize when we have lost alignment with our internal compass and to navigate our lives with purpose, clarity, and passion. But remember that you do not have to tackle this alone. With a coach's help, you can learn to identify these patterns and perhaps even find a kind of humour in them.

Our Privileges

Have you ever considered the privileges you have in life? Let us start by examining some simple aspects.

For instance, are you right-handed or left-handed? While it would be more insightful to hear from left-handed individuals about the challenges they face, we can note a few obvious issues: school desks designed for right-handers, car designs, and various tools and equipment that favour right-handed use. Have you ever thought about how being right-handed is actually a privilege?

Do you live in a place that is secure, warm, and does not leak? Many people still live or work in places that are unsafe or inadequately heated.

Consider if you were to have a disability. How is our environment designed to accommodate various disabilities? Without diving into statistical studies, it is still easy to assume that many designs are not sufficiently inclusive.

Think about how closely your beliefs align with the dominant beliefs in your environment.

Many aspects of our lives that we take for granted actually fall under the category of our privileges. We realize this only when it becomes apparent that we have lost these privileges or when we have gone through the stress of their possible loss. We often accept these conditions as our rightful and normal state, yet they push us into being parts of a system that excludes those who are different.

We become aware of our privileges when we realize we do not have them, and that is when inclusion becomes a topic of concern. If you write with your right hand, you see it as normal and do not take it seriously. The real discussion about inclusion begins when you start speaking about those who are different from you, those who lack the generally accepted characteristics.

I began my career as a well-educated man, much like many white men, not physically disabled or part of a "minority". I entered the workforce fitting a profile that was well received and considered ideal by the dominant culture. Honestly, I never considered myself privileged. It all seemed perfectly normal to me.

We transform our "me versus them" mindset into a collective journey of "us" when we start to recognize what others endure, their needs for support, and how we differ from them.

Realizing this is both good and important, but it is not sufficient. We must act to ensure that these individuals can live the lives they deserve. Picture the process like a moving staircase. You can already walk, and the staircase helps you reach your destination faster. Those without your privileges are trying to ascend on a descending staircase. Observing this situation, you realize that the critical task is not for you to stop moving but to strive to correct the problem affecting the staircase you are not on.

Why do we do this? Partly because it is human nature – the more diverse perspectives we embrace, the better we can collaborate. The more effectively we can get these differing views to work together, the more comprehensive, acceptable, and functional the outcomes become. Systems that acknowledge the needs of the less privileged advance in this way. Conversely, systems that cater only to the strong, dominant, and prevailing often fail to address the needs of the entire society and are less successful both commercially and in terms of their impact.

One way to set aside our privileges is to consider the empty chair at the table. In other words, we should ask ourselves, "What would we do, how would we act if we could hear the voices of those we aren't hearing now?", "How might we change things?", or "Whose voices are we not hearing in the system?"

The more diverse and numerous the viewpoints we hear, the more inclusive we become, and the more effective our work becomes.

What privileges are you living with without realizing you possess them? What does having these privileges exclude from your life? What could become possible if you were to include that which you have been overlooking?

Please Remember. . .

- Having privilege does not mean you are a bad person.
- Having privilege does not mean you lack work discipline.
- Having privilege does not mean you have not faced other types of oppression in life.
- You can have privileges in multiple forms, and it is natural if this feels oppressive.
- Privilege is not a competition about who faces the most oppression.
- Having privilege does not mean you cannot support those who are marginalized; rather, it strengthens your own struggle.
- Having privilege does not mean you do not work.
- Do not feel bad for having privileges.
- Being privileged does not mean that hardworking people cannot achieve what you have.
- Having privilege does not mean you have never faced oppression for your privileged status.

- Being privileged gives you advantages within the dominant culture, but the same status could also create biases within your social networks.

- Having privilege does not mean you are not a unique individual.

- Being privileged is not a situation that is individual in quality; we all participate in discriminatory systems in different ways.

- Pointing out privilege does not mean you dislike or disregard privileged people.

- Highlighting privilege supports making the group you are in fully inclusive.

- Having privilege does not mean your privileges have created a world where you do not face oppression.

- Having privilege does not mean you have it unconditionally.

- Having privilege does not mean there is nothing you can do about it.

- Having privilege means you have choices.

What We Exclude

Are We Aware of What We Exclude?

Sharing emotions that promote functionality, thus generating wealth, abundance, and improved performance through our differences and diverse perspectives, namely the concept of inclusion. So far, so good. However, to foster a culture of inclusion, we must confront three critical questions:

- Is there a tool to measure inclusion?
- How can we increase our capacity for inclusion?
- What are the primary obstacles to creating an inclusive culture?

My research and discussions with global thought leaders in this field have not yet yielded a definitive positive solution to these questions. However, I can offer some encouraging news: by perhaps tackling the issue from the opposite direction, a consensus has emerged that we might find a solution. That is, we can advance our progress on inclusion by identifying what we exclude and by consciously reducing our exclusions through heightened awareness. Why do we exclude and for what? Either to uphold a value we cherish or to protect ourselves against a perceived threat or anxiety. This becomes a coaching issue at both an individual and societal level. When we understand what our reflex to exclude is protecting and we devise a solution that addresses this need, the issue in question then transitions into the realm of what we include. We can give numerous examples for this, starting with ourselves.

To increase our capacity for inclusion, I would suggest reflecting on the following potent questions:

- What am I excluding?
- What is the most challenging aspect for me to be inclusive about?
- Which of my behaviours do I see as resistance to this change?
- What might be the potential threats that cause me to resist?
- Which values or purposes does this resistance serve?
- What would need to happen for this resistance to no longer be necessary?
- What could become possible if I were to be inclusive in this area?
- What actions can be taken to foster an inclusive culture and support inclusive leadership?

Belonging and Independence

Have you ever noticed the distinction between being invited to a place and feeling like you belong there? You have the right to enter in both scenarios, but when you feel invited, you do not truly feel like you belong there. We extend invitations to our colleagues to various places, and therein lies the crux of the matter!

Before I began university, I was uncertain about which department to choose or which university to attend. My father preferred that I study in Ankara, so I needed to find a university there. Being a diligent student, I visited all the departments at METU (Middle East Technical University). In each department, I engaged with professors, department heads, secretaries, and student affairs staff to understand what each department had to offer. One encounter remains vivid in my memory.

I peeked into a partially open door in search of information. The person inside looked up and said, "I was just about to have coffee, would you care to join me?" We shared a cup of coffee together. During our conversation, he asked me a few questions to get to know me better, and we had a pleasant chat. I felt a sense of warmth emanating from that interaction.

The department was industrial engineering, and on that day, I made the decision to join this department. The person who welcomed me was Ömer Saatçioğlu. In that moment, he took the time to make coffee for a high school student who had knocked on his door and personally explained the workings of the department.

It might have been a pivotal moment in my life, or perhaps I would have chosen the same department regardless. The essence lies in the feeling of belonging that

I experienced in that moment. After receiving that warmth and attention, industrial engineering coursed through my veins. Humans are quite simple in this regard. It is not about "You made the cut", "You gained admission", "Congratulations"; it is about feeling like you are a part of something and capturing that warmth.

When we discuss diversity, we often refer to extending invitations; we talk about quotas and statistics. However, inclusion is about the feeling of belonging. To put it simply, in the first scenario, we say, "I'm happy to be here", and in the latter, "I'm happy we are here together". This subtle difference transforms the entire experience.

Belonging is a fundamental concept for inclusion, which we have addressed at the outset when defining inclusion. Tony Robbins lists human basic psychological needs as "belonging" but also "being free", which presents itself as a dilemma; while the other parameter comprises "certainty" versus "uncertainty". Our lives are a constant search for a balance among these four aspects, and when one predominates, it can diminish our enjoyment. This balance may not be the same for everyone.

Consider if there is excessive communal pressure in our lives, too much belonging; we soon crave freedom. While people inherently seek to belong, what is crucial for us is a functional sense of belonging – not a situation where one loves the shackles on their feet, hiding in a place due to fear of uncertainty. That is simply surrendering yourself to something to an extent that it fulfils your desires, instead of being an independent person with adequate free will. In your quest for safety, you have chosen to be shackled to either some place or a doctrine, an ideal, some goal, or some group, to a setting maybe, perhaps an idea.

Belonging and Compatibility

Employers often think employees leave jobs for various reasons. However, the primary reason cited by departing employees is not finding a sense of belonging where they worked. Themes under the umbrella of inclusion also come to the forefront across these reasons.

It is important to understand that feelings of compatibility and belonging are distinct. Compatibility refers to how well parts fit within a whole, often implying a passive adaptation to a predetermined framework or situation. In contrast, belonging is about feeling regarding some kind of a relation; it is an emotion which is experienced when a situation on which one can leave a mark on or to which one can contribute to emerges.

Self-Belonging

It is crucial to discuss our own sense of belonging as well. Just as it is important to feel a sense of belonging to others or an institution, feeling that we belong to ourselves is equally crucial. If we are in any relationship that requires us to deceive ourselves about this feeling, then we are in the wrong place.

Like the feelings of love and being loved, the sense of belonging is a fundamental human need. Thus, we must recognize that our need to feel belonging is intrinsic to us as social beings. If ignored, we expose ourselves to potential suffering and discomfort in our relationships, a finding supported by recent studies on Maslow's hierarchy of needs.

Brené Brown, even in her early works on inclusion, noted that belonging was a significant data point. In her 2017 publication, *Braving the Wilderness: The Quest for True Belonging and the Courage to Stand Alone,*[10] she explores what it means to belong or feel belonging in an increasingly fragmented world.

When it comes to belonging, we should ask ourselves general questions:

- What do we feel when we think about belonging?
- What concerns us about the concept of belonging?

It is crucial to develop a strong sense of self-belonging. We must belong to ourselves to the extent that we are supposed to belong to others. Only then can we truly discover ourselves and share our unique traits with our surroundings and those outside of them.

"Do not change who you are, just be yourself," Brown advises.

How can we belong to ourselves and also to a community? It might seem straightforward, but striving to be part of a whole is complex. Many of us experience various anxieties, torn between trust and distrust, followed by the fears of visibility and invisibility. If these anxieties centre around conforming and being accepted, then this suggests we have not yet achieved a genuine belonging.

To foster a true sense of belonging, we must resist conforming to the expectations or rules of the structure we are trying to integrate with. There is a notable contradiction between "to belong" and "to fit in". Unfortunately, we still grapple with the issues stemming from industrial-era structures and the academic norms established in the 1980s and 1990s.

Organizational charts are typically made up of boxes. Job descriptions are tailored for each box, and afterwards, individuals who "fit in" these boxes are sought. This often forces employees to suppress many aspects of their personalities and individual traits to fit into these prede-fined roles. How can one feel a sense of belonging when squeezed into such confines? Even if this box is a "golden cage", it still remains a form of confinement.

However, when we discuss belonging in the context of inclusion, we refer not to "fitting in" but to actually "belong-ing". It is about being who we truly are in the workplace, carving out a space for ourselves that embraces all our fac-ets, including hobbies, strengths, and weaknesses, beyond the confines of our job descriptions.

We might question why this is necessary from an organizational perspective. The concept of diversity is per-haps most crucial in areas like creativity and resilience. For instance, under stress, during crises, or even in rapidly chang-ing market conditions, it has been proven time and again that we need a reflex to handle situations not covered by our job descriptions. We observed how much damage was done to a brand when a store manager during the Gezi protests decided not to let in demonstrators and closed the shutters. During the pandemic, our lack of knowledge about our employees became glaringly apparent. We saw how their living conditions at home, which were never part of any personnel file, significantly influenced their work perfor-mance. I believe we are moving toward an era where institu-tions – and even cities and countries – that highlight a sense of belonging, where employees can fully express themselves at work, will distinguish themselves.

Of course, Rome was not built in a day. It is a gradual process that requires each stakeholder to breathe life into change and adapt over time.

Sometimes, acting in ways that may conflict with the group we are a part of or developing thoughts they may not agree with can be intimidating. However, taking these risks is crucial to overcoming the fears that hinder our sense of belonging. Only when people truly understand who you are and what you stand for can you achieve genuine belonging.

> "Belonging is not a passive state, but rather demands active participation and visibility. We become truly visible only if we stay loyal to our true selves, because only in this state can we share our ideas and true selves without fear".

Maintaining our sense of self-belonging requires courage. If we fail to preserve this self-belonging, we will find it challenging to develop and deepen our relationships with others. As mentioned earlier, belonging is not a passive state but rather demands active participation and visibility. We become truly visible only if we stay loyal to our true selves because only in this state can we share our ideas and true selves without fear.

Some researchers suggest that many people fail to establish a sense of belonging with their families during childhood, which leads to feelings of loneliness and isolation that can persist into adulthood, resurfacing later in life unexpectedly. "To manage these emotions as adults, it is crucial to continuously reflect on our feelings and look inward. Contrary to the belief that introspection signifies insecurity or weakness, this inward reflection is essential. By examining our feelings, our physical states, our relationships, and our childhood experiences, we can learn to accept ourselves and achieve the sense of belonging we need", Brené Brown explains.

Invisibility and Being Excluded

Invisibility

Invisibility, a term we often use in daily life, comes from the verb "visualize", which means to make visible or create an impression. This concept is crucial for understanding inclusion and the dynamics of belonging.

Almost everyone harbours a natural concern about being visible; thus, invisibility can be one of the most distressing experiences. Feeling invisible within your circle of friends, family, or workplace may lead you to distance yourself from that structure, cutting off communication and connections.

Researchers like Rebecca Neel and Bethany Lasseter, who have conducted valuable studies on invisibility, suggest that feeling overlooked occurs when your ideas are ignored or if you find yourself outside the dominant cultural norms of your group.

There are three types of invisibility:

- Group invisibility
- Interpersonal invisibility
- Representative invisibility

Invisibility labels people, limiting their social engagements and excluding them from being seen as suitable team members or business partners.

To become visible, one must know how to engage effectively. Inclusion is a reciprocal process where all involved must contribute to fostering an inclusive environment. In this context, one must know how to be participatory to be visible. Let us explore this through the scenario of a meeting.

Would the following approach work for you?

I invite you to perform the following exercise. Review the following list and consider each suggestion as a question.

Let us start with an example together: For instance, it says, "Focus on the face and the words of the person speaking". Quite obvious, is it not? We all know this. If merely knowing this advice was enough to change our lives or improve our performance, we would have already implemented it consistently. But presumably, we know, yet we do not do it. What if we rephrase it into a question: "Despite knowing this, what could be preventing me from focusing on the face and words of the person speaking, and what do I need to overcome it?" First, how does this question make you feel? Then, what would your answer be? And importantly, how could you apply that answer in your life?

I have listed the recommendations here. Now, it is your turn to engage with them.

How Can I Demonstrate Participation?

- In meetings or one-on-one conversations with colleagues, show readiness to engage and focus on what they are saying. Small practices can demonstrate your interest in the topic and your openness to communication. For example, avoid distracting yourself with your phone or computer while someone is speaking.
- A good way to show that you value a team member's ideas is by asking relevant questions about their explanations. This not only shows that you listened but also that you take their contributions seriously. It is crucial, however, to ask questions that convey a genuine interest in learning more about the subject, rather than appearing to divert the discussion.

- Showing that you are listening also involves interaction. Do not just ask questions – make suggestions and help develop their ideas.
- Verbal interactions and feedback can energize a meeting or conversation, making it more active and engaging. This way, you can increase the enthusiasm of the person in front of you.
- Your body language and facial expressions are key indicators of whether you are truly listening. Be mindful of these non-verbal cues.
- Focus on the face and the words of the person speaking; make as much eye contact as possible.

What Will I Do to Show I Understand?

- Sticking closely to the topic during conversations is an effective way to demonstrate understanding. Always reference the speaker's words, whether you agree or disagree. Use phrases like "As you mentioned . . .", "At this point you highlighted . . .", and "Similar to how you explained . . .".
- Do not hesitate to use phrases that show comprehension such as "I understand. . ." or "I see. . ."
- Even if you do not like what is being discussed, do not resort to accusatory expressions. Opt for a solution-oriented approach with questions like, "What can we do now?" or "How can we solve this?" instead of, "Why did you do such a thing?"
- Maintain a positive facial expression whether you are speaking or listening.
- There may be times during a meeting or conversation when you need to remain silent. If you cannot contribute by speaking, nodding in agreement can show you are following along and understanding.

How Can I Be Inclusive Towards My Team Members?

- Share your personal experiences. Your way of working or preferences might provide valuable guidance for your colleagues.
- Be consistently accessible and responsive in a friendly and warm manner whenever colleagues reach out.
- Clearly define the purpose of your gatherings in both one-on-one and routine meetings.
- Recognize and thank your colleagues for their efforts and contributions.
- Discourage negative talk about others within the team. If there are no real problems to be solved, explain that such negative talk can harm the group.
- Maintain an open body posture when interacting with colleagues. Avoid turning your back on anyone whenever possible.
- Try establishing relationships with your co-workers outside the confines of the workplace. Be informed about their families, personal problems, or their successes.

How Can I Be Inclusive When Making Decisions?

- Encourage contributions, suggestions, objections, or feedback from your team members. Open dialogue is crucial for effective communication and inclusive leadership.
- Do not interrupt your team members. Show that people can share their ideas during decision-making.
- Explain the rationale behind your decisions to ensure transparency.
- Take your colleagues' criticisms into consideration.

Is It Possible for Me to Appear Both Disciplined and Trustworthy to My Colleagues?

- Do not pick a side in your team's ongoing discussions; act as the conductor and director. It is enough to prevent the personalization of the discussion.
- Make sure your voice is heard and understood when communicating with your team members. Consider diction training if you feel it is not adequate.
- Provide a margin of error for your team. Approach every situation with a supportive attitude.
- Encourage your team members to develop arguments against your ideas.
- Be clear about your views when a failed experience occurs.
- Support risk-taking within your team. Success is not a gain obtained without risk.

Exclusion

We all experience moments of exclusion where we feel disconnected from the environments we inhabit, resulting in discomfort. There are many reasons behind the inability to establish belonging.

Reflect on these questions regarding your personal experiences with exclusion:

- Were you called fat or skinny?
- Were you discriminated against because of your gender?
- Were you discriminated against because of your sexual orientation?
- Were you discriminated against because of your age?
- Were you discriminated against because you or a parent came from another country?

- Were you belittled because you did not have enough money?
- Were you belittled because you lived a wealthy life?
- Were you led to feel inadequate because of a disability?
- Were you discriminated against because of your beliefs?
- Were you discriminated against due to your way of speaking or accent?
- Was your mental health the subject of jokes or ridicule?
- Were you seen as a minority because of the race you represent?
- Were you discriminated against because of your educational status?
- Was your family structure or upbringing perceived as odd?
- Was the relationship you have established with your family seen as strange?
- Was the job you worked at the subject of jokes or ridicule?
- Were you discriminated against because you were employed or unemployed?

The list can be extended much further. If you have experienced such exclusion in these or similar ways, remember that the impact lingers not only within you but also within the environment that perpetuated it. Being inclusive involves the responses to exclusion as much as the exclusions themselves. In your workplace, school, or social circle, do you stay silent when someone is excluded, or do you take action? Consequently, the inclusive lifestyle emerges as a topic which must be considered not only on an individual but also on a societal level.

Notes

1. For my source of inspiration on empathetic disclosure, see David Clutterbuck.
2. Pema Chodron, *The Place That Scared You*, Shambhala, 2005.
3. For the source of inspiration regarding this part, see Brené Brown, *The Gifts of Imperfection*, 2020.
4. *24*, Script: Joel Surnow and Robert Cochran, Production: Real Time Productions and Imagine Television, Fox TV, 2001–2014.
5. Charles Feltman, *The Thin Book of Trust: An Essential Primer for Building Trust as Work*, Thin Book Publishing, 2008.
6. Brené Brown, *Dare to Lead: Brave Work. Tough Conversations. Whole Hearts*, The Borough Press, 2019. Liderlik Etmeye Cesaret Etmek, Transl. Pınar Savaş, Butik Publishing, 2019.
7. Ted Lasso, Creator: Bill Lawrence, Jason Sudeikis, Joe Kelly, and Brendan Hunt, USA, 2020.
8. See website: https://implicit.harvard.edu/implicit
9. For detailed information, https://www.theweathernetwork.com/ca/news/article/shifting-magnetic-north-pole-caught-in-tug-of-war-between-canada-siberia-blobs
10. Brené Brown, *Braving the Wilderness: The Quest for True Belonging and the Courage to Stand Alone*, Random House, 2017.

5

Inclusion in the Personal Development Journey

When we think of inclusion, we always think of being together with those who are different from us, living together, and producing collectively. In this book, too, we have consistently approached the topic from this perspective. However, having an inclusive mindset not only applies to our interpersonal relationships but also grants us a completely new attitude and perspective both in our inner worlds and in our relationships with ourselves.

If we define diversity as that which we have not yet encompassed, then all the new skills, perspectives, talents, knowledge, and equipment that we have not yet internalized can also be approached with an inclusive mindset. In other words, all the innovations we are set to acquire are initially distant and different from us until we internalize them and they become part of our characteristics. Such is the essence of evolution, and our journey of personal development naturally takes shape in a similar manner. If, on this journey, we approach new topics with an inclusive mindset rather than building obstacles for ourselves, we will be met with a much more enjoyable and productive life.

In this section, we will focus on how to use the knowledge and experiences we have gained about inclusion in our own development journey. While doing so, I hope to share some suggestions that will inspire you. I ask that you do not see these as recommendations. I write with the hope that these methods and approaches, which have worked for me, might also inspire you.

• • •

A Memory

From time to time, I recall a period I experienced years ago. I had been appointed as the general manager of a small but successful bank in London. In the existing structure, all business areas were under my responsibility; there was also a supervising British general manager. The bank, though small, was like a laboratory with a significant impact on Turkish banking. We formed a working group in line with the new directives of the European Union, and I was part of that group. We began to discuss the possibility of banks in Germany, England, and the Netherlands coming together. In fact, these banks could merge, and the bank in London could be sold. Indeed, we found a buyer. As you can understand, I signed onto a project that would abolish my own position.

The authority at the time had 12 weeks to make a decision. This meant that for 12 weeks, we could not do anything. We were to just capture a snapshot of the balance sheet.

Personally, I also entered a 12-week period – a period in which my mind was constantly wandering with thoughts. Ultimately, the new owners of the bank would not be conducting business with Türkiye. My accumulated knowledge and added value were related to Türkiye. My daughter had just been born, and we were living in London, a very expensive city. If I could not find a job, we could not stay.

At the end of these 12 weeks, the bank would most likely be sold; and if not, it would close. As I said, I had signed onto a project that left me unemployed. For 12 weeks, I found myself in a position of a complete victim, passive, with an uncertain future. At the peak of my career, I had hit rock bottom.

I truly felt like I was in a well. On one hand, I was a general manager, living in London; what more could I want? On the other hand, my future was uncertain, and I was in a desperate situation.

During that period, I was also attending a coaching training and had a professional coach. My coach asked me, "Rıza, what can you do that is effective in your life?" Thinking about it, I realized that nothing was under my control. At that moment, it would have been very inappropriate to look for a job because they trusted me. I could not look for a job, but if I did not, and the bank closed, everything would be over.

Approaching those who were set to purchase the bank felt like a betrayal to my boss. I felt trapped. I remember, there was a construction site across from our house, with workers busy at their tasks. On my way to work, I would look at them and think, "They have such secure jobs. I don't even know what will happen to me", feeling envious.

Then, I pondered what it meant to be proactive instead of being a victim. Here I was, in London, a Turkish national, with a possibility of becoming Dutch through my wife, but needing to pass a very difficult language exam. For 12 weeks, I had nothing to do; could I make it happen?

Of course, there was another factor motivating me. I loved the Olympics. Though I could not swim well, perhaps my newborn daughter could participate in the future. I wondered, if I passed this exam, could my daughter one day compete in the swimming Olympics? With these dreams, I found sudden motivation. During that time, I took eight weeks of one-on-one lessons, took the exam, and passed. For eight weeks, I got out of bed with a purpose. Instead of dragging myself to work every day, I spent those eight weeks working day and night, dedicated to a full and meaningful goal. I remember every moment.

Life is very interesting. That bank was not sold; it closed. Or rather, the three banks in three different countries merged, with their headquarters in Rotterdam, and they offered me the position of general manager of this newly formed bank. The Dutch Central Bank accepted me as an international director (which I consider a pinnacle in my banking career). But instead of going to the Netherlands, I accepted a last-minute offer from a French bank and returned to Türkiye. In one sense, all those efforts went to waste.

None of my plans from that time materialized, but one truth remained: for eight weeks, I jumped out of bed every morning. I still look back on those days. Whenever I feel challenged or trapped, I draw strength from those memories.

You might wonder, what does this have to do with inclusion? When we think of inclusion, different people come to mind. But at its core, inclusion starts in our own mind.

What am I ready to include in my life?

What will make me leap out of bed in the morning?

It starts by giving meaningful answers to questions such as these. Indeed, the concept of meaning is fascinating as it highlights how our brains inherently construct their own significance.

Growth Mindset

A groundbreaking approach, especially prominent in the field of education, is the growth mindset. I do not need to delve deeply into the entire concept here, but if it resonates with you, you can find the most accurate information by employing numerous sources. I would like to share its general philosophy as it has been beneficial in my work. Carol Dweck, a Stanford University professor, introduced this concept, which is based on a very simple proposition: human brain capacity is not limited; it can develop. So, when we use phrases like finding our potential and elevating our performance to meet that potential, we are making a significant mistake according to Dweck. These phrases assume we have a certain capacity, and reaching it is the best scenario possible. However, Dweck's research shows that the human brain is open to further development at any age. All we need is to believe in this; encourage ourselves and each other; and reward effort, perseverance, and dedication over outcomes.

The survey Carol Dweck suggests provides us with valuable insights. Try it and see what score you get.

After reading each statement, a four-tiered response is expected: Definitely Agree, Agree, Disagree, Definitely Disagree. You have the right to choose one of these four options:

1. Intelligence is a personal characteristic and cannot be changed.
2. You can always change the level of your intelligence.
3. To be good at sports, you must have a natural talent.
4. If you work harder, you can do better in everything.
5. Feedback about my performance makes me unhappy.

6. I greatly appreciate feedback from trusted sources.
7. If you are smart, it naturally comes to you, and you do not need to push too hard.
8. You can always change your level of intelligence.
9. If you are stuck in your own methods and approaches, changing them is not possible.
10. I love learning and applying new things.

The scoring is simple: For odd-numbered questions, "Definitely Agree" scores zero, "Agree" scores one, "Disagree" scores two, and "Definitely Disagree" scores four. For even-numbered questions, the scoring is reversed, with the highest four points for "Definitely Agree" and zero points for "Definitely Disagree". If you score higher than 22, that is great news. If it is under 10, that is a concern! ☺

Developing a Growth Mindset

Handling Challenges

If you find yourself consistently ignoring or postponing challenges, it might indicate a lack of belief in your ability to develop your skills. Essentially, you might be giving up before even trying. However, like any muscle, your capacity to tackle challenges can be strengthened easily. One effective strategy is to start with challenges that you feel more comfortable overcoming. This approach allows you to become acquainted with your emotional responses and reflexes during the process.

Your Relationship with Feedback

How do you react when you receive feedback you do not like? Which emotions are triggered? Where in your body do you feel something? Most of your reactions are likely the result of past experiences. In this context, perhaps you should primarily increase your awareness in this area. However, starting with the cognitive belief that every feedback you receive is an opportunity might constitute the actual first step. Of course, feedback not only provides information about you but also contains valuable insights about the person giving it. Most of us likely compare ourselves when giving feedback to others. Areas of mismatch also become a form of feedback. Therefore, every feedback contains both useful information and some that might not be very useful. As we begin to distinguish between these, our emotional barriers to receiving feedback will likely diminish. I suggest approaching this topic in a way that suits you best. Ultimately, being open to feedback, rather than the feedback itself, contributes to having a growth mindset. This means we become more inclusive of new ideas not because of the feedback we receive but because of our reflex to be open to feedback. As a result, we demonstrate a much more competent and confident stance in the face of challenges.

Our Prejudices About Intelligence

We know there is not just one type of intelligence. Unfortunately, because we are evaluated based on a single metric throughout our educational life, we may have developed notions about ourselves that are not useful at all. There is a saying attributed to Einstein, which you may have seen as a cartoon. Imagine all the animals living in a forest being judged by a single criterion. What would happen? For instance, if they were judged by their ability to climb a tree, a fish would have no chance. But if the criterion changed, say to a competition of swimming across a river. The metaphor is clear, isn't it? Intelligence is like that too. Some studies mention eight different categories of intelligence. How is intelligence categorized? For example, if I mention mathematical intelligence and organizational intelligence, or the intelligence that helps us adapt versus our conceptual intelligence, the difference becomes quite clear.

For instance, throughout my educational life, I was categorized as intelligent because I excelled in every subject, whether it was science, literature, or mathematics. Yet later, I found out that I was struggling with tasks such as organizing a simple meal for three or telling a story effectively to a small group of four. My life was spent trying to excel in areas where I was already good, while also investing in and developing the areas where I was lagging. So the issue is not about being intelligent or not. It is about identifying what you need to develop in yourself with regard to a specific area and finding the resources to do so.

Our Differences in Tolerance to Resistance

The tolerance to resistance I speak of here refers to how long one can persist in the face of challenges before giving up. Those with a growth mindset typically endure challenges longer, increasing their chances of success. However, the core issue here is not just about persistence but about our self-tolerance in the face of challenges.

For instance, what do we tell ourselves upon facing failure? What emotions arise, and what are the costs of avoiding feelings of failure? Or what opportunities do we miss by hastily giving up to mitigate feelings of defeat? People with a higher tolerance for adversity are more likely to seek and receive support, as receiving external support also enhances the likelihood of success. Conversely, those who quit early miss these opportunities. Interestingly, if you demonstrate high resilience in one aspect of life, this trait often extends to other areas as well.

There is also a social aspect to consider. The behaviour of our environment can influence our own; for instance, if those around us give up easily, we might tend to do the same or just the opposite. There is an abundance of empirical studies on this matter. The studies conducted among the minority groups in America have noted that individuals from cultures with a history of intense labour, like rice cultivation, tend to persevere longer. This suggests that perseverance can be both a transitional and a situational trait. This is why, in child development, it is crucial to reward effort and persistence, not just the outcomes. What does not kill us or makes us stronger?

Our Attitude Towards Others' Success

There is a concept called *Schadenfreude*. I could not find a suitable place in the book to insert it. This might not be the right place either, but it could be beneficial to approach the topic from the opposite direction. It is a word of German origin. I do not know which culture it belongs to as a concept. In summary, it means taking pleasure in someone else's misfortune. Dreadful, yet true all the same. In fact, it is a phenomenon we encounter a lot nowadays. In polarized societies of our day, individuals and even whole communities have surfaced which derive pleasure from the suffering of their opponents. Maybe they had always been here, but now they have become visible through social media. At this point, however, our focus is on the diametrically opposed. Namely, the reaction to someone else's success. If others' achievements trigger deep and sincere feelings pertaining to a lack of self-confidence, anxiety, and self-doubt in you, then you may still be in a place far away from a growth mindset. The growth mindset, conversely, includes a reflex for getting inspired and being empowered by the success of others.

Our Attitude Towards Failure

The lexicon of the growth mindset does not include the word "failure". Rather, any undesired result is treated as a prime opportunity for learning. Reflecting on personal experiences, when posed with the question of what counsel I would offer my younger self from 30 years ago, one poignant piece of advice stood out: "Fear not rejection". Historically, I equated rejection with failure, yet each rejection is, in fact, an educational opportunity – quite a challenging notion to internalize. The emotional toll of rejections has often been hard on me. This has gradually led me to circumvent scenarios where I might face denial, thereby curtailing opportunities for personal expansion in these fields.

However, human beings are complex. While I avoided potential rejections in some areas of my life, I confidently faced challenges in others. For instance, I would tackle difficult chemistry problems in front of a class without fear of failure. And when I did fail, I would just shrug it off with a laugh, ask for support, and later study and overcome the challenges the subject posed. But I lacked the courage to approach a girl I was interested in just to say a couple of beautiful remarks. I fell to the ground countless times, and I injured nearly every part of my body. Yet I never could take a risk with skiing. In my own right, I think I had a pretty good basketball career. I have carried over many good memories from those days, some of which I still reminisce about. But skiing on winter vacations remains a torture for me. I wonder how you are processing these scenes from my past as I depict them. What is your attitude in the face of failure? Does it shift depending on the context, as mine does? And if so, what advice would you give yourself about it?

A Different Attitude Towards Learning

Curiosity, while potentially leading us into predicaments, is fundamentally vital for fostering a growth mindset. For those who hang their diploma on the wall and conclude their journey of education there, the growth mindset is a very alien concept. Consider the professional whose office walls are adorned with diplomas and certificates – testaments to a commitment to continuous learning. This scenario might initially impress; it showcases a dedication to personal growth and knowledge acquisition. However, a critical observation might reveal that for some, the wall represents not an ongoing journey but a completed tableau. Does it then convey a growth mindset or something else? For instance, I recently visited a doctor friend of mine who is prominent in his field and was featured on a television programme that very day. That seemed like a perfect opportunity for me to drop by for a chat and perhaps get a quick health check-up. His office, situated in a leading hospital, boasted several framed diplomas and certificates. Notably, a few frames remained conspicuously empty, which must be a symbolic gesture to his ongoing educational journey, indicating potential areas of future expertise yet to be determined; I liked that very much. But interestingly, he was oblivious to the significance of these empty frames. The empty frames were just that, frames that happened to be empty. We found this amusing and laughed. There was no need to rack one's brain over to such a degree. We are ready to learn if something is required. But if not, we too deserve to stop and rest for a while from time to time.

The Need to Prove Ourselves

The need for external validation some of us need is quite influential, is it not? For me, it has always been so. While it did provide an initial motivation for me, over the years, I have come to recognize its constraints. Seeking confirmation, appreciation, and approval from our surroundings can severely limit the risks we are willing to take. Consequently, we become deprived of the "thick skin" that embarrassment would bring us. Those with a growth mindset can feel the urge to be validated as well. However, in their case, it is not the validation from their surroundings that matters; it is the appreciation from within that takes precedence. This distinction often roots back to our upbringing – whether we were reared under the critical eye of exacting parents or in an environment of excessive praise. Both conditions can foster a dependency on external validation, which may complicate the journey towards self-discovery and hinder our ability to pursue paths fuelled by our own convictions, rather than sail on by the winds of others; the harbours we arrive at, not our own, but belonging to those who provide the applause for us. In this way, we may find ourselves having drifted far away from the growth mindset, living not by our own right but as someone else.

Our Different Attitudes Towards Effort

What matters is not so much what happens to us; rather the important thing is how we change by the responses we give to life's challenges and the residue they leave behind within us. This epitomizes what is known as *reflective practice*. This perspective prioritizes the journey as much as the destination. In fact, the journey carries even more significance because it prepares us for other journeys. Concentrating solely on results can trap us in a cycle of short-term satisfaction, which ultimately robs us of the many opportunities offered by the long term.

I can illustrate this with an example from basketball. For those who mature in height swiftly, their early basketball positions are often near the basket – like the post or pivot – leveraging their height advantage. This yields considerable satisfaction for them as, relative to shorter peers, they can score more effortlessly and easily secure rebounds due to their stature. However, while doing this, they neglect to develop other skills such as shooting from a distance or dribbling. As years go by, everyone grows taller, and some may reach a very tall height, while those who grew tall early may lose their advantages in the following years. This mirrors my own experience. When I started playing basketball in middle school, I already stood nearly 1.80 m tall. With a 20 cm advantage over my closest rival, my role on the court was clear. Yet, as years progressed and I capped at 1.90 m – a height which my peers have surpassed – my initial benefit diminished, earning me the moniker "clumsy giraffe". When I reached the end of high school, I was still playing on the team but had fallen out of the starting five. Confronted with a pivotal choice in my sophomore year – either to forsake basketball or learn to dribble and shoot from distance in order to move to the forward position – I opted for the latter. For a semester, I went to the gym nearly every night, often practising alone. Of course, my position did not change immediately, as there was no other centre player to take my place, so I was stuck in my old position. But there is something I'll never forget. There was a tournament taking place among high school teams of the American bases in Türkiye. For some reason, our high school also participated. We lost the last game and came in second. But in the game before the last, against the İzmir base, I had moved myself from the post position to forward, and I broke my personal record for rebounds and total points, reversing my role as the typically least scoring player; that day I scored the most points. This confidence carried me through college. I was not on the team, but I had a lot of fun experiences during spring festivals. Later, when I went to America for my graduate studies, I did not venture much into sports. But my real peak came during the years I did my MBA in France. I joined the university team as a forward. That year I had the experience of being the best player both in our league and the school team.

Learned Optimism

Learned Optimism is a book I deeply admire, which perhaps stands as Martin Seligman's finest work. This seminal book, rooted in an extensive, long-term study, compellingly illustrates that individuals with an optimistic outlook on life generally experience longer, higher-quality, healthier, and more fulfilling lives. The stark divergence between optimists and pessimists does not manifest until they reach their forties, but as they advance in age, the difference becomes profoundly significant. For those captivated by the topic, I heartily recommend not only this book but also Seligman's other works, notably *The Optimistic Child* and *Flourish*.

In this discourse, I shall refrain from delving extensively into the foundational theories or reproducing Seligman's diagnostic tool, which comprises 48 questions designed to assess one's optimism level. Those interested may access this evaluative tool online at www.rkacademy.biz.

The important and beneficial thing for us, at this juncture, is how optimism is defined in this context. Seligman delineates optimism across three dimensions.

First Dimension: *"Permanence"*

We could also call it persistence or continuity.

Individuals prone to relinquishing their optimism, who capitulate readily under adversity, typically harbour a belief that they are inherently culpable for negative events and outcomes. In contrast, optimists perceive the causes and repercussions of adverse occurrences as transient. For instance, where a pessimist might declare, "Diets invariably fail", an optimist would counter, "Diets falter only when one frequents restaurants too often". Rather than lamenting,

"The boss is an absolute nightmare", they might suggest, "The boss is just having a bad day". Instead of an accusation like "You never communicate with me", an optimist would observe, "You've been unusually quiet recently". You must see the difference, of course. While one believes the situation is to be permanent, the other attributes a condition, a time, and/or a circumstance to the adverse conditions.

Experiencing failure can momentarily induce feelings of helplessness in anyone, akin to a visceral punch or a fall from a bicycle. Such incidents can indeed inflict acute pain and a sense of fatigue and debilitation. However, for those who view these setbacks as circumstantial, the accompanying distress is often fleeting and varies considerably, much like the weather's ever-changing nature, as assured by the cyclicality of seasons; this too shall pass.

Conversely, when fortune smiles to their faces, the optimist's response also distinctly contrasts with that of a pessimist. Faced with positive developments, optimists entertain the possibility of their permanence, while pessimists anticipate their swift dissipation. For example, a pessimist might attribute a good day to mere luck, whereas an optimist considers themselves generally fortunate for it. Rather than attributing a singular success to effort and struggle, optimists might ascribe it to inherent talent, further bolstering their motivation through a sustained belief in their continuous success, provided it remains grounded in reality. As opposed, pessimists, convinced of the fleeting nature of success, might find themselves increasingly demotivated.

Second Dimension: *"Pervasiveness"*

The first dimension is closely related to time; the second dimension pertains to the environment and interpersonal interactions. When faced with severe setbacks in one area of life, pessimists tend to lose their enthusiasm and energy across all other areas. Conversely, optimists maintain their positive attitudes elsewhere. For example, a person who is terminated from their job might descend into a career-related depression, but optimists manage to shield their social and familial relationships from this negativity. They continue to engage in their hobbies and other interests that connect them to life and human relationships robustly.

Consider the case of a student who feels unfairly treated in one class. This student might declare, "All teachers are always unjust", reflecting a pessimistic view. However, an optimistic student would attribute the issue to that particular teacher only, avoiding sweeping generalizations about all educators. This dysfunctional thought pattern is also evident in scenarios like encountering a misdiagnosing doctor and concluding, "All doctors are like this", or having a poor holiday experience and pondering to themselves, "All vacation spots are always disappointing". After a break-up, thinking, "All men are the same". Optimists avoid such overgeneralizations that can further darken their worldview. Instead, they approach each new experience with renewed enthusiasm and an open mind, preventing past negative experiences from blunting their appetite and excitement.

In line with the previous dimension, optimists are more prone to positive generalizations when good outcomes arise. Achieving well in a class might lead them to think, "I am smart", allowing positive occurrences to elevate their vitality and zest for life.

The encompassing theme here is "hope".

Ultimately, the perspectives on permanence and pervasiveness shape our outlook towards life with either a sense of hope or hopelessness. Those with a pessimistic view on these dimensions struggle to find hope, whereas a more optimistic stance significantly enhances one's capacity for hopeful living.

Third Dimension: *"Personalization: Internal/External"*

How we personalize events is the third dimension of optimism. When adversity strikes, individuals may either internalize the blame or attribute it to external factors. Those who habitually blame themselves and accept personal responsibility for negative outcomes often struggle to maintain an optimistic outlook on life.

Briefly summarizing, it may seem that those who shirk personal accountability, attributing positive outcomes to themselves while blaming others for negatives, and adopting a "this too shall pass" mentality during hard times, expecting perpetual good fortune, might be living in a delusion. This perspective has merit. Yet the absolute opposite approach is equally unhelpful. Individuals who consistently fault themselves for failures anticipate continual disappointment, believe that success is dependent on externalities, view themselves as perennial victims, and are less likely to take proactive steps to change their circumstances. Societies filled with such individuals are not likely to look forward to brighter futures.

In essence, optimism can be seen as a form of inclusion. By not cooping up some place, rejecting the passive or victimized mindset and embracing life with the vigour that optimism provides, we can hope that individuals will set sail for a slightly better life every day. Without such an outlook, the inevitable outcome is either personal or societal despair.

Whether or not this process will transition towards a constructive and developmental path hinges on the principles discussed throughout this book. I pen these lines with the conviction that by discarding our biases, stereotypical views, and learned helplessness, all the while heightening our awareness, and through being determined to respect those who are different from us within dialogues based on mutual understanding (empathy) and trust, we can establish a foundation for societies where feelings are not neglected, functional emotions are protected, and relationships become nourishing. It is my belief that what awaits such societies will invariably be futures with greater prosperity.

6

Inclusion Development Model in the Institutional Context

S ince inclusion is such an important topic, it is evident that we need to increase our inclusion capacity both individually and institutionally. So how will we go about achieving this?

In this section, we introduce a method designed for this very purpose. Initially, you will perform a situational analysis, as per the first stage of our method, using what we have termed *the inclusion barometer*. Then, taking these assessments into account, you will make use of our five-step strategy roadmap to navigate the insights you have gathered. Finally, considering that this is a process, we propose an approach that is sustainable and yields continuous benefits.

We are talking about a dynamic process that is continuous, not static. In other words, we are discussing a phenomenon that should be approached with the "infinite game" paradigm, which is always ongoing and has no end, rather than with the "finite game" approach, which has defined end-points. Finite games are characterized by set rules, fixed players, and definitive outcomes, where there are clear winners and losers. Most conventional games fall into this category. On the contrary, in infinite games, the rules, participants, and even the scope of the game are ever changing, with no clear beginnings or ends. For instance, we often use the example of a company's performance, which can be considered as a finite game. Public companies issue a balance sheet every quarter, but all companies do so annually. The players in the industry are ranked in different categories, and the criteria for success and failure are clear. Market valuations fluctuate, credit opportunities are determined, and even the employee and customer preferences are swayed in response to these metrics. The economic game that companies play today can be seen as a finite game. However, commerce and economic life have existed throughout human history and will persist indefinitely. They have no true beginning or end, the participants and rules continuously evolve, and the significance of a win is minimal, as the game continues on regardless. Therefore, your approach to business will change depending on whether you see your professional life as a finite game or an infinite one. What matters is playing the right game in the right place. As long as you adopt a functional approach that suits your expectations, preferences, and needs, the game will seem meaningful and even enjoyable to you. Otherwise, you risk encountering issues like cognitive dissonance, alienation, exclusion, and the burnout syndromes detailed throughout this book.

In this context, inclusion is a phenomenon that should be considered an infinite game. It has always existed and will continue to do so, sometimes taking centre stage and sometimes receding into the background. Its rules and approaches may evolve, but as long as humanity endures, so will the phenomenon of inclusion. Therefore, it requires a strategic approach distinct from the typical diversity initiatives we often see. While creating an action plan for diversity, defining key performance indicators (KPIs) and generating continuous analyses and reports are standard practices; there is a prevailing tendency to treat diversity as a "finite game". However, inclusion does not fit neatly within such confines. Although you can set your own success criteria in the method we propose, ensure these criteria emphasize sustainability and continuity. What is crucial is not merely what takes place but the impact it leaves behind, the residue on your psyche, and the transformations it facilitates with regard to your perspective. Please adopt this mindset when considering inclusion.

Regarding strategy, I would like to share a recent experience.

Recently, I was invited to a television programme. They had prepared a special report. The findings showed that due to increasing rental costs, businesses were moving from major city centres to more peripheral areas and even preferring to operate from multiple smaller centres instead of a single large headquarters. In essence, the questions posed were "What does hybrid working promise in the face of rent and inflation?" and "What should companies do in this situation?" I was expected to provide insights on employment, the economy, and related topics. I said:

> *As long as we are preoccupied with urgent and important tasks, we feel correctly positioned. The business climate in our country typically operates with a fire-fighting reflex. There is a prevailing thought that everything is urgent, and by focusing on the important things, we will do the right thing. However, we must abandon the habit of managing companies by looking in the rear-view mirror. It is imperative that leadership, including top management and controlling stakeholders, devotes attention to issues that are significant yet not pressing. To answer your question, each institution needs to develop an inclusion strategy tailored to its unique circumstances. Consider the sequential crises we have faced; initially the pandemic, followed by inflation, energy crises, refugee influxes, demographic shifts, social unrest, forest fires, and earthquakes, floods, and now escalating rents pose the latest challenge, with the overarching climate crisis looming over us. The challenges we encounter are only set to escalate. Crucially, the task at hand is determining which conditions, perspectives, lifestyles, technologies, and solutions we are prepared to embrace.*

After sharing these thoughts, I surmised that they might probably not invite me back, yet shortly after, they sent a message to my phone, and I received another invitation. It appears that our message is beginning to resonate.

It is one thing to articulate this, but implementation is an entirely different beast. How might we prevail then?

First, we need to understand, reflect on, accept, internalize, and implement all the concepts and principles mentioned in this book. Then comes the stage of making a situation assessment. For this purpose, you can tailor and utilize the corporate inclusion barometer we propose according to your specific circumstances. Ultimately, by following the five-step strategic roadmap outlined in the subsequent pages, you will be able to develop your institutional inclusion capacity.

Let us proceed one step at a time.

Institutional Inclusion Barometer

The most effective way to determine whether an inclusive culture exists in a community is by asking the individuals who make up that community how they feel. This model is predicated on the approach that "Perception is reality".

You might already be acquainted with the life wheel exercise. It starts with deciding on the headings under which we will conduct a situation analysis in any given area, looking at life as a whole. Once these aspects are defined, an evaluative score is assigned to each: a 0 indicates complete dissatisfaction, desiring change throughout, whereas a 10 reflects utter contentment, with everything aligning perfectly with one's desires. These scores are then plotted on a circular diagram, resembling a wheel.

Drawing inspiration from Linbert Spencer, whose methodologies I greatly respect and employ in my coaching practices, I propose a modified version of the **life wheel** exercise. Assess the following questions on a scale from 0 to 10, where 10 signifies "perfect, wouldn't alter a thing, exactly as I desire", and 0 represents "abysmal, I would change everything; nothing is as it should be":

TOPIC	SCORE
My teammates / colleagues listen to me.	
Even when I have unconventional ideas, I can express myself and speak without fear of consequences.	
My teammates / colleagues provide me with information and explanations about what I need to do.	
In team / organizational conversations and group jokes, jargon and abbreviations are used to an extent that does not make me uncomfortable.	
I receive thanks and appreciation for my work.	
I am allowed to support my teammates within the given tasks and responsibilities.	
I am informed about what is happening.	
Time is allocated for me.	
The organization / team invests in me.	

The initial trio of queries is vital for gauging inclusion on an individual level in terms of visibility, auditory engagement, and presence. The subsequent trio sheds light on the senses of belonging and recognition, while the final three relate to how well an individual can perform at their best and their satisfaction with the opportunities provided for them to do so. The fifth and seventh questions can also be attributed to line mangers' ability to give feedback, listen to, and to inform their team.

By plotting your responses on a life wheel, you gain insights into your personal inclusion experience. Consider selecting one category to further explore what your ideal score might be, how it compares to your current score, what changes might bridge the gap to your ideal, and the potential avenues to achieve it.

These inquiries can be customized to suit the unique needs and characteristics of your institution. Assigning numerical values to the responses and calculating an overall inclusion score are also a feasible option. Perhaps more importantly, such a survey can serve as a useful tool for developing an idea of what needs to change in terms of inclusion within the institution and for shaping a transformation map in terms of both attitudes and behaviours.

Upon conducting this survey, what did the results tell you?

As an institution, it identifies the important issues you need to focus on, while also providing each individual with an opportunity to conduct a self-assessment.

Subsequently, these findings can be deliberated in small group workshops, where participants discuss the implications of the results and contribute meaningfully with their interpretations to the five-step strategy roadmap development exercise slated for discussion in the ensuing segment.

Development Strategy for Institutional Inclusion Capacity

To bolster the capacity for inclusion within institutions, a framework developed by EMCC Global can serve as a useful guide.

Here is a brief overview of the model:

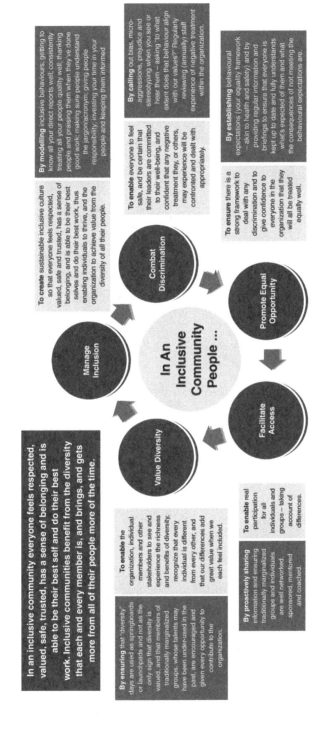

In an inclusive community everyone feels respected, valued, safe, trusted, has a sense of belonging and is able to be their best self and do their best work. Inclusive communities benefit from the diversity that each and every member is, and brings, and gets more from all of their people more of the time.

In An Inclusive Community People ...

- Manage Inclusion
- Combat Discrimination
- Promote Equal Opportunity
- Facilitate Access
- Value Diversity

To **create** sustainable inclusive culture so that everyone feels respected, valued, safe and trusted, has a sense of belonging, and is able to be their best selves and do their best work, thus enabling individuals to thrive, and the organization to achieve value from the diversity of all their people.

By **modelling** inclusive behaviours; getting to know all your direct reports well; consistently treating all your people quality well; thanking people and praising them when they've done good work; making sure people understand the jargon/acronym; giving people responsibility; investing your time in your people and keeping them informed

By **calling** out bias, micro-aggressions, prejudice and stereotyping when you see or hear them – asking 'to what extent does that behaviour align with our values?' Regularly reviewing (annually) staff experience of negative treatment within the organization.

To **enable** everyone to feel safe, and be certain that their leaders are committed to their well-being, and confident that any negative treatment they, or others, may experience will be confronted and dealt with appropriately.

By **establishing** behavioural expectations (your equality framework – akin to health and safety) and by providing regular information and briefings to ensure that everyone is kept up to date and fully understands what's expected of them and what the consequences of not meeting the behavioural expectations are.

To **ensure** there is a strong framework to deal with any discrimination and to give confidence to everyone in the organization that they will all be treated equally well.

To **enable** the organization, individual members and other stakeholders to see and experience the richness and benefits of diversity, recognize that every individual is different from every other, and that our differences add great value when we each feel included.

By **ensuring** that 'diversity' days are used as springboards or launchpads and not as the only sign that diversity is valued, and that members of traditionally marginalized groups whose talents may have been under-used in the past, are encouraged and given every opportunity to contribute to the organization.

By **proactively** sharing information and ensuring traditionally marginalized groups and individuals are well networked, sponsored, mentored and coached.

To **enable** real participation for all individuals and groups – taking account of differences.

The fundamental philosophy on which this work is built is that in an inclusive community, everyone feels respected, valued, trusted, and safe, has a sense of belonging, and believes they are doing their best work. An inclusive community benefits from the diversity of its members and often produces more benefits than what all the members individually gain.

What steps can be taken to achieve this goal? This model will guide us through this process step by step.

Managing Inclusion

Objective

> *To cultivate and maintain an inclusive culture where everyone feels respected, valued, safe, and trusted, enabling a sense of belonging, self-realization, and the ability to perform at their best. This ensures success for all and enables the institution to derive value from its diversity.*

How will we accomplish this? Let us systematically address the subheadings provided by the model, creating an action plan for each to increase awareness and enhance development:

Modelling Inclusion Behaviours Inclusion thrives on positive examples. It is crucial to identify, showcase, and promote these instances to reinforce inclusive behaviours. This should be a collaborative endeavour involving all members of the community, rather than directives issued solely from higher management. One effective method is to gather examples of inclusive actions through an e-mail address or a suggestion box. These examples can then be widely disseminated among the community, particularly through those actively engaged in promoting inclusion.

Questions we will consider:

- How can we pinpoint behaviours that foster inclusion?
- How can we filter and select exemplary instances?
- How can we establish a group of "inclusion ambassadors" to actively engage in this area?
- How can we enhance the visibility of inclusive behaviours?
- What strategies can we employ to model inclusive behaviours?

Getting to Know Your Members Well One of the best lessons the pandemic has taught us is that we did not know our colleagues and members who bring life to our institutions well enough. It became apparent how inadequate the information in personnel files is in terms of inclusion processes. Even the information we record in terms of diversity turned out to be so limited, didn't it? However, knowing a person involves foreseeing how they will react under different circumstances. Their values, dominant emotions shaping their lives, thought patterns, and paradigms will help you better understand why they react in particular ways in different circumstances. ... Workshop activities that bring these to light and facilitate their sharing, thematic sharing rooms, chat opportunities will help us to know each other better.

Questions we will consider:

- How can we design experiences and environments for our members to get to know each other better?
- What else can there be besides chat rooms, hobby groups, thematic sharing opportunities?

- What alternative shared activity or discussion formats could prove beneficial?
- How might we effectively manage and embrace emerging differences during these collaborative activities?

Treating Our Members Equitably Well Addressing a subtle yet critical nuance, we recognize that treating different individuals with uniform fairness does not necessarily enhance our capacity for inclusion. Such an approach can leave many feeling inadequately acknowledged. Equity aims to bring everyone to the same concrete outcome, yet when we focus on individual feelings, the principle of treating each person "equitably well" becomes pertinent. This is not about uniformity but about ensuring each individual feels sufficiently valued and included. Articulating this is straightforward; implementing it, however, is an art form with considerable complexity. Our endeavours in this domain yield fruit only when they stem from an appropriately nuanced perspective, fostering a sense of being treated equally well over mere equity. EMCC statement defines equality as "treating people equally well" and contrast that with "treating people the same".

Questions we will consider:

- How can we treat each other equitably well, taking into account all our differences?
- What strategies should we employ to accurately assess needs and situations as they evolve?
- Based on barometer results, which groups or individuals require more focused support in what area?
- What would make us feel more equitably treated?
- How can we compile good examples and share them with all our members?

Thanking and Praising for Good Work   This topic, simple in concept yet intricate in practice, perhaps owes its complexity to anthropological and evolutionary predispositions of the human brain towards identifying and focusing on areas in need of enhancement. This inherent bias towards recognizing deficiencies applies to ourselves, our loved ones, and broader society. Traditionally, the onus has been on individuals to pinpoint their weaknesses and seek improvement – a narrative deeply ingrained in our educational systems and how we are raised. So it should not come as a surprise that we have shaped the systems of our creation in a similar manner as well. However, as discussions throughout this book suggest, the focus is shifting from the individual to the collective – crafting societies where diversity is not merely tolerated but celebrated for enhancing communal well-being.

Instead of zeroing in on personal shortcomings, the new paradigm encourages the formation of teams that complement each other's strengths, fostering environments where members genuinely enjoy collective engagement. Advances in artificial intelligence, demographic changes, and technological developments underscore this imperative. The key lies in reflecting the good sides of one another, recognizing and promoting each other's strengths and successes. Reflecting on the earlier analogy of the chicken-egg experiment, it becomes evident that while isolated high performers may falter over generations, groups that uplift each other achieve sustainable success, emerging over generations. This approach emphasizes celebrating each other's virtues and fostering more harmonious communities, which enriches emotional well-being and minimizes the sterile, ineffective competition that so often prevails.

Questions we will consider:

- How can we make the good examples visible?
- How can we design systems that effectively recognize and praise contributions, enhancing morale across the board?
- What systems can be put in place to provide recognition and appreciation without fostering harmful competition?

Helping to Understand Jargon and Abbreviations   One of today's paramount challenges is comprehending the significance of our lives within communities that share meaningful objectives. As we have mentioned before, "What's all this even for?" A life which we bestow with meaning upon the discovery of such meaning and a career nourished by the fulfilment of its purpose from which we also end up drawing strength. All this begins by harmonizing our language – not merely the diverse tongues of different nations but rather the jargon and abbreviations that, despite a common language, often obfuscate mutual understanding. Jargon, a formidable tool within the elitist circles, serves to alienate broader society and erects arguably the most nonsensical of barriers to inclusion. While it may grant members of a group a sense of exclusivity, it ultimately promotes a counterproductive culture of exclusion. It deters newcomers from joining, alienates them until they assimilate, and fragments us into isolated enclaves within a globally connected society. Indeed, while abbreviations enhance linguistic efficiency and facilitate swift comprehension among subject matter experts, they also carry some inherent risks. At times, an abbreviation may stray from its original intent or become obsolete as contexts and paradigms evolve, while the language remains static. Hence, if jargon and abbreviations are essential for the effective functioning of a community, it is crucial to make these accessible. We must strive to elucidate such terminology to new members and even the broader public whenever feasible, ensuring inclusion extends to all stakeholders.

Questions we will consider:

- How can we become aware of the jargon and abbreviations we use?
- How can we compile a comprehensive list of jargon and abbreviations?
- In what ways can we elucidate the functional use of jargon and abbreviations?
- How can we eliminate their use as a tool of exclusion?
- What measures can we take to make the meanings of jargon and abbreviations accessible to all?

Appropriately Sharing Responsibility   Inclusion blossoms not just through visibility and being heard but also by sharing responsibilities. Indeed, the genesis of most everything often begins with making demands, sometimes on behalf of ourselves, sometimes for others. Thus, we should approach inclusion by actively embracing responsibilities. The success of an inclusive culture within an institution cannot hinge solely on one individual or department. It is not the exclusive purview of the senior management or any particular manager. Instead, it requires creating a milieu where all stakeholders convene, sharing responsibilities tailored to the institutional and individual contexts. This necessitates identifying and addressing any cultural elements or corporate values that may obstruct this process and understanding that these are not under threat. Our own privileges often serve as covert barriers in this shared responsibility. The greater our awareness of these barriers, the more adept we become at distributing responsibilities.

Questions we will consider:

- Which of our values conflict with inclusion?
- What elements in our culture hinder inclusion?
- Which of our values might prevent us from taking responsibility?
- How might our privileges hinder us from taking responsibility?
- How can we encourage others to take responsibility?
- Which responsibilities can we undertake together?
- What good does shared responsibility do for us?
- How can we identify areas that need improvement in responsibility sharing?
- How can we periodically check for areas that need improvement in responsibility sharing?

Making Time In coaching training, we master the art of posing powerful, effective questions – a skill that seems straightforward but hinges on where we direct our curiosity. We aim not to satisfy our own curiosities but to enhance the awareness of the individual before us, often employing open-ended questions. Consider the query, "How are you?" – a daily nicety. Occasionally, I respond earnestly to those who ask, though the answer is complex. I must introspect, comprehend my state from various angles, and articulate it. As my response lengthens, I notice the asker's regret for initiating such a deep inquiry. Thus, in everyday interactions, we shirk from asking meaningful questions to avoid lengthy dialogues for which we lack time. Similarly, discussions about inclusion require deliberate time allocation, mental preparedness, and focus to be fruitful. It is quite difficult for dialogues on inclusion to be productive without making time.

Questions we will consider:

- What do we need to make time?
- What is preventing us from making time?
- Why can't we make sufficient time for meaningful dialogues and actions towards inclusion?
- When we realize such a concept of time, how does this realization affect our internal sentiments?
- What do we focus on that makes time cease to be a constraint?

Sharing Information   The non-disclosure of information can be likened to a corporate malady. With the advent of technology and the creation of structures that foster shared value through the dissemination of knowledge and skills, this issue has diminished but remains pertinent. We must consistently ensure that sufficient information is shared to augment our corporate inclusion capacity. The prevailing question should not be "What happens if I share this? Why should I share it?" but rather "What is preventing me from sharing?" By identifying these barriers, we can devise solutions and transform sharing into a spontaneous reflex.

Why does sharing information matter? Reflect on the inclusion barometer survey. Our sense of belonging is intimately tied to our comprehension of ongoing developments. Being well informed is the first step; without this knowledge, it becomes challenging to grasp the collective objectives that unite us. Absence of information fosters a sense of invisibility, altering our feelings towards an environment we fail to understand, which can initiate feelings of alienation.

Certainly, the deliberation over the extent and intent of information sharing is crucial. When an overwhelming volume of information is shared, it can paradoxically lead to alienation. Take, for example, an experience from my tenure as chairman of an institution. One of our vice-presidents, who was performing exceptionally, regularly sent exhaustive, page-long reports to all other board members. However, these reports were so extensive that I observed they were largely unread, leading to frequent admissions in meetings of "But I didn't know about this!" countered by the vice-president's frustrated retorts of "But it was all detailed in the reports!" This scenario highlighted that our method of disseminating information was ineffective. The person unaware of the updates felt out of the loop, and the one who had diligently reported felt deeply let down. What, then, is the solution? As I often advocate, "a human being is primarily an emotional creature that occasionally thinks". Thus, our approach to sharing information must also be emotionally intelligent. Information necessary in a cognitive context should be presented simply and clearly, akin to a vehicle's dashboard, yet the emotional implications of each datum should be scrutinized. Details that aren't displayed on this metaphorical dashboard but are of significance to the individuals should be incorporated, whereas unnecessary information should be pruned to prevent overload.

Systemically, this metaphor should now resonate more clearly. But how do we translate this into individual relationships, where no tangible dashboard exists? Here, organizational charts can serve as a useful metaphor – not the boxes but the lines between them, which truly vitalize an institution, particularly elements that constitute the corporate culture. The missing element in these diagrams often involves the information flow: who should inform whom to ensure everyone is content and performs effectively. In personal relationships, the extent of information shared is typically dictated by the dynamics established within those relationships.

Questions we will consider:

- Who requires what information from us to ensure they feel included and effective in their roles?
- Who should not be informed about which information, and why not?
- How does the information we share affect the recipients emotionally?
- What do they miss out on if we do not share?
- What other values of us does sharing threaten?
- What information do we want to receive and for what purposes?
- Who can we ask for this information?
- How can we ask for it?
- What is the best approach when responding to requests for information?
- How can we establish a system within the institution that promotes easy sharing and handling of information requests?

Standing Against Discrimination

Objective

To ensure that everyone feels secure, assured that their safety is being monitored and confident that any negative attitudes they or others may encounter will be addressed and prioritized.

To achieve this, we will meticulously address each of the model's subheadings one by one, preparing an awareness-raising and developmental action plan for each, asking the following questions:

- How can we recognize partisanship, micro-aggressions, and biases?
- How can we confront them?
- How can we ask ourselves what to do so as to ensure that behaviours within the institution align with our core values?
- How can we make this review process continuous?

Identifying and expressing awareness is the most critical issue. In fact, we all feel it when we experience micro-aggressions. Or when we are exposed to favouritism. Or when we realize that prejudices are putting up a barrier. It emerges as a palpable feeling. The vital step thereafter is to transform this feeling into a thought and articulate it. Especially if unconscious biases are at play, or even if stereotypes are involved, the other person may have unknowingly reflected this back to us. And often, because of this, when we express these feelings to the other person, we may be met with a reaction. Therefore, instead of confronting this one-on-one, it might be more effective to create sharing circles. One possible, systematic approach could be the following:

First stage: We could implement an "inclusion buddy" system. We might arrange for every member to participate in triads, serving as each other's inclusion buddy. These small groups could confidentially share their experiences of micro-aggressions, partisanship, and biases, avoiding the mention of specific individuals or timings. Such initial sharing would likely cultivate a sense of belonging.

Second stage: Subsequently, we could form inclusion circles comprising no more than 15 members, where all our members convene monthly. Each participant from the initial triads would join a different circle, ensuring comprehensive engagement across these meetings. Here, experiences would be shared anonymously, and the group would collectively deliberate on how these behaviours correspond with our values. Rotating circle members systematically each time for at least a year would facilitate all our employees in listening to and understanding their colleagues better.

This methodology is merely one suggestion, and I am confident that you could devise even more effective methods. Herein, it is essential to share experiences, address them openly, and foster new communication practices.

The essence of the challenge lies in confrontation. In this process, the person who perceives themselves as a victim might, knowingly or unknowingly, exhibit a micro-aggression towards the individual who elicited this sensation. The roles of victim and aggressor can interchange, and even the system might be manipulated. Consequently, rather than responding hastily to these accusations, discussing the issues collectively, raising awareness about what is transpiring, and concentrating on group dynamics would yield substantial benefits.

Resisting discrimination is a crucial matter that can aid institutions perceived to possess robust cultures in overcoming their corporate myopia. Traditionally, recruitment systems emphasized fitting within the corporate culture. Recent controversies have highlighted that hiring individuals who mesh well with the corporate ethos actually reinforces strong social pressures and an exclusivity reflex, which, over time, challenges institutions' efforts in fostering inclusion. It is imperative that our shared values not only unite us but are articulated in a manner that champions our collective aspirations and honours our differences. What other systems of resistance to discrimination could there be?

Promoting Equal Opportunity

Objective

Fostering a robust institutional framework, addressing all forms of discrimination, and instilling confidence in equal treatment for all within the institution.

Questions we will consider:

- How can we ensure that our members understand what is expected of them and the consequences of not meeting these expectations?
- By respecting behavioural expectations (within the framework of equality, health, and safety) and regularly sharing information, how can we ensure that our members stay up-to-date on these issues?

In fact, what we are discussing is to focus on the means of incentivizing our members and keeping them in such a state continuously so that the possibilities detailed under the first item, "Managing Inclusion" can become realities. Here, an adage comes to mind which goes a little something like this: "Some rights are not given, they are taken". In this context, it is paramount to encourage our members to assert their rights to inclusion, which can only flourish in a milieu of trust. Thus, I advise revisiting the segment on "Trust" previously discussed, where we have explored trust-building from the angle of relationships on the individual level. At this point, it is imperative to consider the application of these trust elements within an institutional framework. To reiterate, here are the main headings:

B (Boundaries): For trust to develop, it is essential to establish clear boundaries, which can be thought of as a set of rules encompassing guidelines and actions. If it is not clearly established who is responsible for what actions and where these actions are to take place, we are likely starting off in an unhealthy situation.

R (Reliability): Okay, we are positioned to meet certain expectations. But can we achieve the same level of performance consistently? Will they follow through on their commitments? When faced with conflicting expectations and rules, can we still count on them to consistently fulfil our expectations?

A (Accountability): Will they take responsibility if the expected performance is not achieved? Moreover, will they assume responsibility if a loss occurs? Will they remain present during unpleasant situations and share in the consequences with us?

V (Vault): Who will share what information with whom? Will my privacy be respected? Will they share information about me or our shared situation with others? What should remain confidential and what can be disclosed? Will they use what they know in a way that could harm me?

I (Integrity): Will they stay true to the ethical framework that united us? Will they betray the principles and values we share? In difficult situations, will they compromise these important principles for situational solutions?

N (Non-judgement): Can I interact with them in complete transparency without being labelled or pigeonholed? Can they assess me and the situation without judgement, accepting me as I am? Naturally, I would feel disinclined to stand alongside a person who judges me from various other angles, apart from the common subject which unites us.

G (Generosity): Will they interpret any action, word, and intention in the most positive way and be especially generous emotionally in their attitudes and behaviours towards me?

I think here, there is no need to further elaborate these headings at a corporate level, as they require tailored application to fit the unique conditions of each institution. Should you require further assistance in navigating these processes, my guidance remains at your disposal.

Facilitating Access

Objective

> *To act proactively in information sharing (and indeed, why not engage when there's a need for information) and to facilitate the introduction of colleagues from "traditionally marginal groups" to networks, potential sponsors, mentors, or coaches.*

Questions we will consider:

- How can we recognize differences in access?
- Considering these differences, how can we ensure all our members participate in opportunities for development, profile enhancement, skill improvement, and so on?

Or to ask it in other words:

- What invisible barriers might there be in our institutions?

Corporate culture, while streamlining operations, often induces a form of corporate blindness. Proclaiming "This is how we do things" inherently excludes those who might approach tasks differently. This exclusion is not limited to individuals; it often extends to innovations, particularly in realms like new technologies, workflows, internal communications, and compliance, manifesting as significant obstacles. When new ideas are seen as "teaching new tricks to an old dog", a critical resistance point is revealed.

Our approach mirrors the Gestalt change paradox: identify resistance and engage with it. Listen to it, comprehend its purpose, recognize its value, and then collaboratively explore how change can be implemented without undermining the values it upholds. Once resistance is addressed, change naturally ensues.

However, identifying entrenched "glass walls" within the culture is seldom straightforward. As diversity wanes, so too does the demand for inclusion. In such cases, it is crucial to actively enhance diversity and reassess our capacity for inclusion. Simple strategies include recruiting new organizational members or boosting internal mobility to foster transitions between departments.

My esteemed mentor, Professor Hawkins, describes culture as "what you stop noticing after 90 days in an institution". Culture becomes invisible as it is internalized, much like fish that do not notice the water they swim in or living beings that are not aware of the air they breathe unless there is a change (e.g. in smell, pollution, temperature, or colour). The same notion applies here as well. Thus, the most effective method to gauge our capacity for inclusion is to encourage feedback from new members or those who have transitioned to new roles, allowing them to share their observations. This facilitates easier identification of new access requests and existing barriers.

Valuing Diversity

Objective

> *To use diversity days not just as symbolic gestures of valuing diversity, but as springboards, to encourage and celebrate the talents of members from traditionally marginalized groups, whose abilities have not been adequately utilized in the past, and to ensure that they are provided with every opportunity to contribute meaningfully to the organization.*

Questions we will consider:

- How can we ensure that the institution, our members, and other stakeholders see and experience the richness and benefits offered by diversity?
- How do we acknowledge that each individual is unique and that when we feel inclusive, we recognize that our differences add significant value?

The critical point here is to see awareness efforts focused on diversity, not as static moments captured in a photograph but as images in a filmstrip transitioning to the next scene. In other words, every diversity-focused effort should be made with planning for the next frame in mind. It should be designed as a celebration but with a focus on **"What will we celebrate next time?"** – probably the most fundamental question with regard to diversity.

As we determine and internalize the answer to this question, we will naturally return to the first point with renewed energy and desire to better manage inclusion. Ultimately, common goals bring organizations together. The value our members place on their work is directly proportional to the meaning they find in it. That is why we say purpose-driven companies stand out. As we acknowledge the value generated by the synergy of diversity and inclusion, our enthusiasm for, opportunities within, and resources dedicated to this process will invariably expand.

7

Final Words

So How Shall We Design Our Futures in Light of These Developments?

Stanford University faculty members Dr Evans and Dr Bennett have adapted their methodologies in product and service design towards the field of designing life itself. Although their studies had actually begun during my time on campus, being an engineering student who was primarily focused on achieving success in my own field of study, I did not have the chance to fully grasp the significance of human relations, personal development, and leadership for a successful career in business life. Some 30 years of time have passed since then, and somewhere along the line, I guess I have come to my senses. It was just before the pandemic. I had been given the opportunity to host the "D. Life" lab events both in İstanbul and in Amsterdam. Coincidentally, D. Life was where Evans and Bennett had been furthering their research.

They would often say, "There is no GPS to guide us through life's journey", highlighting that in our ever-changing world, it was impractical for us to set a fixed point for our futures and confidently start our journey on a path we had deemed as right. Their preferred and self-advocated way to navigate life was to always move towards the "next best port". Studies now indicate that only a fifth of the people can articulate what their passion is, and these results contradict the conventional wisdom of "Always find what you are best at and focus on it to design your future". The saying is considered to be flawed now; the approach it embodies has been contradicted by the recent scientific findings. Instead, they emphasize that it never really is too late to create a more fulfilling life by identifying the activities which boost our life energy without necessitating any major changes to our daily routines.

They assert that, nowadays, "meaning making" has gained more importance than "making money". During a related discussion with partners from IRC (International Global Executive Search Partners) in Amsterdam, they mentioned that relocating a manager from Mexico to Europe was more feasible than moving a manager between the cities within Europe. And on a flight, a businessperson sitting next to me was lamenting about how a seven-day week was insufficient for him, but in Leiden, almost everyone at their subsidiaries was only clocking in four days a week. He seemed to still have some trouble with accepting such a reality.

The secret lies in wherever we find the meaning in our lives and, of course, in the added value we create. Unfortunately, in this context, we are entering a period of time wherein the level of geographic disparities will most likely be on the rise as even though it offers numerous opportunities worldwide, technology will also be exacerbating the divide in value created across different regions on a global scale.

If We Were to Give Advice to Ourselves from the Future

I think the best way to prepare for the future is getting to know ourselves a little bit more and then to embrace technological change. If we find ourselves in a state of resistance, we should lean in and lend an ear, so that we may notice specifically in which way we are trying to assist ourselves with this resistance. After all, by resisting, we will only make it harder on ourselves; so it just might benefit us to locate its source and attempt to grasp the reason behind it.

Consider the taxi drivers and the tourism managers, resisting technology in an era where there are more than five billion smartphones worldwide. It is without doubt that they will eventually end up defeated by applications such as Uber, Lyft, Booking.com, and AirBNB. The incumbent players face a problem of wealth, namely the problem of losing it, as their investments, which hold a certain amount of value, now carry an obvious risk of depreciation. But what has this got to do with the taxi driver or the tourism manager? Why are they worried? Well, they will both face obstacles of differing kinds due to technology, and these differing obstacles will require separate solutions. But still, they are marching into the swamp together, and every time they use force on another workingman, in every instance they try to hide behind shields of law and statutes, they sink a little but more, a fact they will never be able to change.

But indeed, the same is true for all of us. That is why the term "uberization" has already made its way into the literature. We are all afraid to lose our jobs and, along with it, the reasons which justify our existence. Every passing day witnesses the emergence of a new method able to create the added value we do in our workplaces instead of us. Competition is moving beyond the limitations of geography. The real added value never really leaves its position of being located right at the centre of institutions. New technology firms seem to create very little in terms of added value outside the cities where their headquarters are located. Previously, new technologies would create multileveled chains of added value; their emergence would witness the formations of distribution, sales, representation, maintenance, and post-sale services. This is not the case with the contemporary platform economies. And if distributed ledger technologies and incremental production systems meet expectations, it will be the most educated population which suffers the greatest losses. And on top of all that, we have also encountered ChatGPT and other AI applications similar to it. In a report by Goldman Sachs, it was stated that, with applications such as these entering our lives, 300 million job losses were expected in North America and Europe alone. This will only serve to further the income inequality, summarized as the "1% problem" to the point where it becomes much, much more visible. Social revolt movements such as "Occupy Wall Street", "The Arab Spring", and "Gilets Jaunes" will proliferate rapidly while the political arena will witness extremist views gaining more and more support.

So What Is to Be Done?

- All stakeholders have responsibilities to avoid being losers in this change.
- Public authorities should understand this development well and accept it, establishing an ecosystem where this

change can flourish. Collaborations should be created with the leading regions of this change at municipal levels.

- Leading institutions in the business world should support their employees, universities, secondary education institutions, and entire supply chains with the means that they will require in order to further themselves regarding the technological transformation. Instead of maximizing today's profit figures, they should invest in resources that will build tomorrow.
- Individuals should transform all their fears and anxieties into a motivating drive and develop themselves with an insatiable appetite and will with regard to new skills, technologies, and ways of working.
- We will also create spaces of collaboration, production, and living where we can feed off our differences, feel safe, experience respect, practise mutual understanding, accept others, and be accepted as we are.

The roadmap for individuals is already somewhat clear. Many studies list the personal qualities people will require the most within the new order as follows:

- Sense making
- Social intelligence
- Original and adaptive thinking
- Cross-cultural competency
- Computational thinking
- New media literacy
- Interdisciplinary work
- Design mindset

- Cognitive load management
- Virtual collaboration

It does not sound very daunting, does it? Essentially, we are entering a period where our human qualities that make us who we are will be of great use to us.

Rumi once remarked, "Why sentence yourself to the dungeon's embrace when the universe bursts forth with abundance? The door stands wide open". While Shams Tabrizi is attributed with the quote, "How do you know what's down is not better than those above?" That is to say, throughout history, change has always been a constant. Even though it may feel like it was us who got the short end of the stick, how can anyone know what countless others had to suffer through, or, for that matter, if what will befall countless more? I believe the important thing is to not get stuck in the truths of yesterday, which brought us to the place where we are now but rather acknowledging that they might, indeed, be hindering our progress, much less constituting enough to take us forward. Then, we might actually start to discover the positive aspects of this change and proceed to prepare ourselves in that direction.

It is my hope that in spite of the daily chaos we inhabit, we might still be able to facilitate a process whereby taking the initiatives necessary would be enough for us to circumvent taking our place among the losing side of this magnificent transformation.

8

Sources for Inspiration

From Japanese Culture

Concepts borrowed from the Japanese culture can help us improve our lifestyles and may be advantageous in establishing order.

Japan is known as one of the best places to live, largely because of its profound understanding of the ideal way of life and its purpose. This inspiring culture represents a remarkable fusion where ancient Eastern philosophy meets modern Western life, creating a unique harmony. It is a culture where East meets the West. And in this context, I believe Japan can inspire us in many ways.

I would like to start here with an approach summarized as *Wa kei sei jaku*.

Wa: Harmony.

Kei: Respect.

Sei: Purity.

Jaku: Peace.

Currently, there are endless discussions taking place around sustainability almost to no end, and we are continuously reviewing our lifestyles and business practices in terms of circular economies. But there is a missing dialogue, namely "What exactly are we aiming to sustain?" Upon deeper examination, it becomes apparent that what everyone seeks to maintain is a lifestyle they believe is suitable for themselves and their loved ones. However, these individual desires frequently lead to conflicting goals, and when combined together, they seem to exceed the finite resources of the globe.

Eastern philosophy offers an alternative perspective – living in harmony, in particular, with ourselves, our communities, nature, and the universe at large. Additionally, if we were to achieve such a harmony, we also would not need to choose what to sustain, as all stakeholders would be in a state of balance, harmoniously supporting another's opinions.

To further inspire you, I would like to share these profound Japanese concepts, each rife with so much depth and meaning, that a book alone would not be able to cover just a single one of them:

- **Oubaitori**

Never compare yourself.

Each person blooms in their own time and way.

How would it be possible to avoid judging oneself in relation to the path of another?

- **Kaizen**

Continuous improvement.

Small changes accumulate and create the significant difference.

How can you continually strive to improve every aspect of your life?

- **Wabi-sabi**

Embrace imperfections.

Nothing lasts long, nothing is complete.

How can you accept your own imperfections and those of others?

Where can you find beauty in imperfection?

- **Gaman**

Maintain dignity under duress.
Emotional maturity and self-control are essential during challenging times.
How can you foster more patience, perseverance, and tolerance in your life?

- **Ikigai**

Knowing your reason for being.
What is it that makes you leap out of bed in the morning?
And how can you add even just a pinch of this to your life?

Imagine something you are good at and passionate about, and that the world needs – answer each three, how would you discover what lies at the intersection?
There is actually one more additional question as well: For which of these would the world be willing to pay you?

- **Shikata ga nai**

Accept and let go.
Some things are beyond our control.
How can you recognize things you cannot change, accept them, and move on?

- **Shu-Ha-Ri**

Do not be wasteful.
Everything deserves respect and gratitude.
How can you better appreciate and conserve the resources around you?

• Kintsugi

Imperfections are a matter of beauty and part of the whole. Indeed, they are the ornaments that beautify the journeys we embark on.

How can you go about repairing the cracks in your life using "gold"?

• Omoiyari

Life is better when we care about others.

How can you show more thoughtful consideration and compassionate interest towards others?

The Athena Doctrine

Years ago, at a meeting of the EU, to which we have attended to discuss economics, one speaker highlighted that a significant barrier to Turkey's entry into the EU was the disparity in women's employment rates.

During my banking career, I have worked alongside women who resumed their careers after a hiatus, and I have consistently been impressed by their performance. I believe in distinguishing between feminine and masculine roles rather than making distinctions based on gender. In professional life, it is more practical to focus on functional traits, many of which are increasingly recognized as feminine qualities.[1]

In *The Athena Doctrine*, researchers John Gerzema and Michael D'Antonio presented findings from their two-year long study which globally involved over sixty thousand participants. They began by identifying more than 120 character traits observed in human nature which were prevalent in the business realm. Secondly, 32,000 participants were asked to categorize these traits as either masculine or feminine. Finally, another group of 32,000 evaluated how beneficial these traits are in the business world, particularly for leadership, success, ethics, and happiness. The findings were quite interesting.

Traits that are now seen as essential for successful leadership, such as flexibility, patience, intuition, passion, collaboration, loyalty, reasonableness, future-oriented thinking, expressiveness, and empathy, were predominantly identified as feminine. Conversely, traits considered masculine, such as aggression, analytical thinking, independence, resilience, decisiveness, and pride, were not favoured for effective leadership.

Addressing the issue as a "men versus women" dichotomy tends to create more exclusion, friction, passive aggression, and resistance. It is disheartening that many successful women felt compelled to adopt traditionally masculine behaviours to advance in their careers. However, as I have been claiming for years, for a balanced and harmonious work environment, it is crucial to recognize that each individual can develop and utilize both masculine and feminine qualities effectively in their roles. This perspective has been reinforced by my experiences in inclusion work over the years. Fostering inclusion for some at the expense of others invariably leads to active or passive resistance, as observed in recent events. Nearly all advancements in female employment made over the last decade were erased during the pandemic. Yet, in families where men and women share life responsibilities equally and genuinely, balance persists. Conversely, individuals, institutions, and societies that begrudgingly accepted active female participation in the professional setting often reverted to the traditional roles at the first sign of stress.

In this context, rather than viewing the advancement of women's employment and their roles in business and social spheres as a competitive struggle that excludes others, a more sustainable and successful approach would be to cultivate feminine qualities in men as these qualities are increasingly recognized as enhancing leadership in today's socio-economic climate and would result in them naturally promoting a demand for gender-balanced professional environments, which would also constitute a more successful and long-term method. Hence, it is crucial to support not only women but also men in developing these traits.

Additionally, it is also possible for us to impose our own barriers beyond those pertaining to the external. Often, the greatest impediment to a life led fully ends up being our own limiting beliefs and learned pessimism. It may also be claimed that for some women, their biggest obstacles are created by their inner voices, which may be echoing the societal norms and expectations ingrained over time. Perfectionism also emerges as an adversary to women as reflected in their inner voices.

Rather than resisting, we should welcome an era characterized by the internalization of inclusion all across the individual, family, institutional, and societal levels. By doing so, we would be paving the way towards a future that is both more prosperous and peaceful for everyone.

Resilience

Thinking of bouncing back, and bouncing ever higher.
To keep going regardless of any defeat.
Refusing to give up.
To resume.

We all recognize it, yet resilience is a concept frequently overlooked in times of abundance, prosperity, and development. In Turkish, this resilience is expressed through various terms, but the one I find most fitting is "yılmazlık". The reasons for this choice will become more apparent as you read on.

I wish to share some insights from an article I compiled on this topic, emphasizing the need to view resilience not just individually but also through institutional, social, and ecological lenses. In our highly interconnected era, seeking fragmented solutions within isolated boundaries proves inadequate. If our discourse centres on sustainability, then the resilience strategies we adopt must also be sustainable.

Resilience is deeply intertwined with sustainability. I prefer the Turkish term "yılmazlık" because it conveys notions of "staying in the game" and "enduring despite all changing conditions to fulfil the purpose of existence".

Our living conditions are undergoing rapid changes, making it challenging to resist or adapt to these shifts. Since controlling the rapid changes around us is often out of our reach, we must learn to devise more appropriate solutions. This involves establishing new institutions, organizations, and systems better equipped to manage disruptions, operate under varying conditions, and transition smoothly between states. We might also need to rethink and redesign existing structures. But gaining a deeper understanding of "resilience" could be one of our most valuable endeavours.

Globally, experts across seemingly unrelated fields such as economics, ecology, political science, informatics, and digital networks – from scientists to policymakers, technology developers to corporate leaders, and activists – are all grappling with the same critical questions:

- What causes a system to collapse and be replaced by a new one?
- To what extent can a system digest change and maintain its integrity and purpose against it?
- What features make a system adaptable to change?
- In an era of continuous disruptions, what can we do to better absorb the shock of change for ourselves, our communities, corporations, economies, societies, and the entire planet?

In this discussion, "resilience" emerges as a pivotal field. This emerging field is developing generalizable understandings aimed at crafting social, economic, technical, and commercial systems that can anticipate disruption, renew themselves when predictions fail, and reorganize to sustain their fundamental purposes even amidst radical changes.

The strategies that involve ensuring sufficient resource provision in a specific system, diversifying inputs, and gathering reliable and real-time data on operations and performance, or making system components more autonomous to prevent the disruption in one part from affecting the entire system are all resilience strategies. These strategies are applicable at every scale, from entire civilizations to communities, institutions, and individual lives.

Since resilience carries different nuances across various disciplines, defining it precisely can be complex. Here's how resilience is characterized in several fields:

- In engineering, it refers to the extent to which a structure, like a bridge or building, can return to its original form after a disturbance.
- In emergency response, it is the swiftness with which critical systems restore normalcy following disruptions like earthquakes or floods.
- In ecology, resilience describes the capacity of an ecosystem to resist or recover from destruction.
- In psychology, it denotes an individual's ability to effectively manage and recover from trauma.
- In business, resilience often relates to the activation of data or resource backups to ensure operational continuity amidst disasters, whether natural or human-made.

Although these interpretations highlight different scenarios, they all pivot around two central elements of resilience:

- Continuity
- Recovery

Utilizing terms from ecology and sociology, we can thus define resilience as the ability of a system, whether it be a company or an individual, to maintain its core purpose and integrity amidst significant changes.

To illustrate this concept, consider a metaphor often used in resilience research. Visualize observing a landscape filled with imaginary hills and valleys extending in every direction. Each valley symbolizes a potential variation of your current state, each possessing distinct characteristics, opportunities, resources, and challenges. The peaks represent critical thresholds or boundaries that, once crossed, transition you into a neighbouring valley. This new environment might facilitate ease or pose challenges, and in some scenarios, adapting to this new reality could be extremely difficult or outright impossible.

From an inclusion perspective, integral to the theme of our book, we must consider what we need to include in order to effectively navigate the upheavals brought about by external changes.

In everyday life, numerous sudden and severe disruptions can radically alter your existing circumstances, propelling you across a threshold from an old reality into a new one. You might experience a flood or drought, be invaded, or suffer an earthquake; you might find yourself nearly alone in your valley or lost in a crowd where you cannot find space. Similarly, your business might grapple with economic downturns, energy shortages, technological shifts, or unexpected scarcities in essential materials. Such environmental unpredictabilities can shatter prior assumptions, often making a return to former conditions unfeasible. This necessitates acceptance of the new status as the norm.

Cultivating psychological resilience involves enhancing your ability to withstand forces that could displace you from your preferred "valley" while simultaneously broadening your options should relocation become necessary. This dual capability, described by scholars of psychological resilience, involves maintaining adaptability – continuing to fulfil one's primary functions while adjusting to new circumstances – and is crucial in our times of unforeseeable disruptions and uncertainties.

Of course, there are many ways to expand the range of living spaces you can inhabit. You might sustain life in resource-scarce environments by minimizing your material needs or make do with what is available by becoming more resource-efficient. Innovations in technology can provide escapes from conventional constraints, adapting tools intended for one environment to another, or learning collaborative strategies with new community members can mitigate the struggles faced in new settings.

The resilience of an ecosystem, economy, or community can therefore be fostered in two primary ways: by strengthening resistance against being driven beyond critical thresholds that could cause lasting damage and by preserving and broadening the spectrum of viable environments in which the system can effectively adapt when such boundaries are inevitably crossed.

The quest for organizational effectiveness, the constraints imposed by ecological systems, and the profound interconnectedness defining our era have propelled certain approaches to prominence. These methodologies, whether applied on macro or micro scales, consistently feature in the discourse on resilience.

Key strategies that underpin resilience include establishing frequent and effective feedback loops, fostering dynamic organizational reconfigurations, and developing mechanisms to counteract excessive integration and break damaging linkages. Principles such as diversity, modularity, simplicity, and clustering are integral to these strategies. They provide a comprehensive framework for evaluating the resilience and vulnerabilities of substantial systems such as urban centres, economic structures, and essential infrastructures that are foundational to contemporary society. With these tools at our disposal, pertinent questions arise:

- How can we craft more effective feedback loops that closely align our actions with their impacts?
- How can we reduce dependence on critical yet scarce resources or enhance the modularity of our infrastructure?

Typically, resilient systems avoid catastrophic failures through preemptive strategies that avert potential hazards, detect unauthorized changes, minimize and confine damage to components, diversify resource inputs, operate within constrained capacities when necessary, and reorganize to buffer impacts.

No system is flawless; in fact, quite often, the opposite is true. The concept of "perfectly imperfect", one of the most valuable gifts from Japanese culture, resonates here, suggesting that systems that seem flawless are often most vulnerable, whereas a dynamic system that occasionally errs is more likely to be durable. Resilience, akin to life, is inherently disorderly, imperfect, and sometimes inefficient, yet it persists.

New scientific research suggests that personal, psychological resilience is more common, more developable, and more teachable than previously assumed. This is because the foundation of our resilience lies not only in our beliefs and values but also in our character, experiences, values, genes, and most importantly, our habits of thought – the habits that we can develop and change.

When our discussion broadens to consider the resilience of groups, new themes demand our attention. Among these, the critical roles of trust and cooperation stand out, alongside the capability of individuals to work collaboratively when the situation requires it.

Diversity, too, is crucial within the resilience framework and represents one of its foundational pillars. Whether referring to the biodiversity of coral reefs or the cognitive diversity within a social group, enhancing the diversity of the components within a system furnishes it with a broad spectrum of responses to potential disruptions. The challenge, then, is to ensure that this diversity is coupled with mechanisms that maintain effective cooperation across varying conditions.

It has been observed that robust social resilience is often found in strong communities. However, the strength here is not derived from wealth. Resilience does not stem solely from a community's resources or the robustness of its formal institutions. Instead, resilient communities often depend on informal networks characterized by deep-seated trust, which plays a critical role in addressing and rectifying disruptions. While top-down approaches to fostering resilience frequently falter, embedding these efforts within the fabric of everyday relationships significantly enhances the likelihood of success.

Discussing the role of effective leadership within the context of resilience, it becomes clear that in resilient communities or institutions, there is often a distinctive type of leader at the centre or close to the centre of the group. These transformational leaders, irrespective of their age or gender, are pivotal in linking system components and aligning different networks, perspectives, information systems, and agendas. Throughout their leadership, they facilitate coordinated governance, promoting a collaborative response to crises by both formal and informal institutions.

As I have consistently emphasized, our leadership must extend beyond mere individuals or the delineated roles within organizational charts; rather, we should focus on the relationships between individuals – or, from another perspective, the lines connecting the boxes on those charts. While the boxes themselves remain unchanged, the transition of individuals occupying them can provoke considerable shifts within an institution. However, if the connections between individuals and their functions are robust, the institutional climate remains stable even amidst such transitions. In this regard, effective leadership for resilience must prioritize these connections and lead through relationships. This approach naturally underscores the importance of inclusive leadership and positions inclusive leaders as pivotal figures.

The elements that constitute the foundation of social resilience – beliefs, values, habits of thought, trust and cooperation, cognitive diversity, strong communities, transformational leadership, and coordinated governance – collectively create the ecosystem that nurtures social resilience. When these components are considered holistically, they reveal new methods for strengthening the resilience of communities, institutions, and their individual members.

So how do we fortify our personal resilience amidst life's inevitable challenges?

Well, the concept of resilience is a strong lens with which we are able to re-evaluate the critical issues. Consider the following applications:

- Business planning: How do we shape our corporate strategy to cope with unforeseen circumstances?
- Social development: What strategies can bolster the resilience of vulnerable communities?
- Urban planning: How do we ensure the uninterrupted operation of city services during a disaster?
- National energy security: What combination of energy sources and infrastructure will best equip us to withstand inevitable disruptions?

The myriad examples available vary widely, yet they share a common thread when viewed from an individual perspective – our personal situation, our position within the broader scenario, essentially, our individual resilience.

In all mentioned sectors, the concept of resilience compels us to confront the possibility – and perhaps the necessity – of failure, acknowledging the limitations of human knowledge and foresight. It presupposes our ignorance of complete answers, our susceptibility to surprises, and our propensity to err. Although we champion resilience as an aspirational goal, it is not intrinsically virtuous; terrorists and criminal organizations also exhibit resilience, driven by the same dynamics previously described. There are valuable lessons to be gleaned about resilience from both benevolent and malevolent entities.

However, the resilience mindset does not merely advocate for a defensive posture against uncertainty and risk. Rather, it promotes adaptability, agility, cooperation, connectivity, and diversity acceptance, fostering a transformative way of engaging with the world and deepening our relationship with it. Transitioning from a static mindset to a growth-oriented one that welcomes innovation is crucial. While enhancing our likelihood of surviving impending crises is vital, the advantages of resilience transcend mere survival, equipping us to more adeptly handle numerous, lesser challenges that erode our daily resilience.

Sustainability and Resilience

Here, we pivot to discuss "globalization". Despite its apparent advantages, globalization exacerbates interconnections and hidden dependencies among all forms of global assets, which can accelerate the erosion of adaptability.

Globalization typically enables the optimization of specific variables, such as resource extraction or consumption, but it also permits the delay or obscuration of environmental feedback related to such optimization.

Globalization also intertwines vastly differing systems – financial transactions occurring in milliseconds, social norms evolving over years, and ecological processes unfolding over millennia. As these systems interact more intensively, their potential for disruption escalates, amplifying the speed, sources, and impacts of disturbances, paralleling increases in personal, community, institutional, and environmental distress when disruptions occur.

Despite the noble aim of aligning human activities with planetary sustainability, the practical application of sustainability may be approaching its limits. This evolution is natural; like many social concepts, sustainability has its life cycle, and at 40 years old, it has outlived many others. Originally, the scope of what was considered "sustainable" expanded continuously, perhaps now reaching a plateau of diluted significance.

More critically, from my perspective, sustainability grapples with two fundamental challenges: firstly, its aim to establish a singular equilibrium is often at odds with many natural systems that thrive not on static balance but on dynamic health. Secondly, the strategies sustainability advocates to manage escalating disruptions are relatively limited. In contrast, a resilience-oriented approach offers a broader, more adaptable, and contemporary set of ideas, tools, and methodologies. As uncertainty and instability persist, resilience strategies may increasingly supplement or even supplant traditional sustainability frameworks.

To illustrate the potential shift from sustainability to resilience, consider the following thought experiment.

Imagine gathering all individuals concerned about a major global disruption, such as irreversible climate change, or another significant future crisis. We place these individuals metaphorically in a single vehicle, excluding those who deny the severity or existence of climate change. Now, envision this vehicle approaching a precipice symbolizing the point of no return for climatic alteration.

Initially, those in control of the vehicle are the *mitigationists*. Their immediate reaction is to halt progress: "Turn back!" they insist. "Apply the brakes! Or at least, ease off the accelerator!" At this stage, their approach likely represents the most prudent course of action.

However, when the initial interventions by the mitigation-focused group fail to prevent the vehicle's approach towards the precipice, and even as the brakes are applied, there emerges a point where the vehicle might still slide off the road. At this critical juncture, another group assumes prominence – these are the *adaptationists*. They argue, "It might be wise to install airbags and deploy parachutes", acknowledging that despite efforts, crossing the threshold remains a possibility. This stance, too, holds moral and practical merit under the circumstances.

The transition between these viewpoints often spans generations, characterized by vigorous debate. Initially, those advocating for mitigation may accuse the adaptationists of defeatism – of prematurely conceding to inevitable disaster. Conversely, as the situation grows increasingly dire, the adaptationists may critique the mitigationists for futilely expending resources in an attempt to avert what they perceive as unavoidable.

Traditionally, the sustainability movement has focused predominantly on risk reduction – a necessary and effective strategy. Yet, as the spectre of irreversible global changes looms larger, there has been a discernible pivot towards adaptation, emphasizing the importance of resilience. This shift is evident across various domains, including global economics, public health, poverty alleviation, and corporate strategy, each susceptible to potential future risks.

This evolution in strategy does not imply a resignation to disaster or an abandonment of hope. Rather, the resilience framework suggests a nuanced, supplementary approach to traditional reduction tactics. It advocates for a redesign of our institutions and a revitalization of our communities, urging innovation and proactive experimentation. It calls for bolstering societal capacities to anticipate, withstand, and recover from disruptions, all while continuing efforts to mitigate these threats. By adopting resilience-focused strategies, we buy time to undertake more profound, long-lasting transformations. Extending the metaphor further, it is akin to retrofitting the proverbial car – not only with better brakes but with wings, fundamentally altering the scenario to the extent that traditional brakes and parachutes might become obsolete.

The growing complexity and vulnerability of our global systems have elicited varied social and political reactions. Among these responses are the thoughts of the group labelled as "Icarus", who advocate for scaling back human activity – slowing down, simplifying, and adopting local solutions. Their strategies include reducing reliance on the hydrocarbon economy by embracing backyard farming and local energy production. Many within this group view an impending societal collapse not with dread but as an opportunity to foster a more balanced, less consumptive, and ultimately more fulfilling lifestyle.

While supporters of Icarus advocate for a return to a smaller scale of life, members of the "Manifest Destiny" group argue that it is unfeasible to go back and that we must find ways to cope with inevitable problems. They argue that the existence of billions of affluent and profligate humans, alongside billions aspiring to similar wealth, and yet more billions yet to be born, dictates a relentless expansion and exploitation of Earth's resources. While recognizing the problematic nature of this trajectory, they maintain that it will spur more efficient innovations, many of which have already begun to emerge, and may eventually harmonize human activity with the planet's ecological limits.

Thus, the challenge becomes one of accepting our significant role on Earth and leveraging technological advancements to minimize our inevitable impact on the world. Imagining a lifestyle that is in sync with both ourselves and nature could reduce the ecological footprint of our desires, allowing the planet a chance to regenerate. "Since we cannot diminish, we must instead enhance our adaptability" could be a guiding principle. However, a pivotal question remains: For whose benefit and in what manner should our intellectual and technological capacities be directed?

At this point, I think the most significant barrier we face is the pervasive "instant gratification" syndrome that has taken over our lives, especially affecting young people and the newer generations. Nature inherently operates over time – human gestation lasts nine months, flowers bloom seasonally, and leaves turn yellow and fall when their time comes, enriching the soil. In contrast, urban lifestyles have disconnected many from these natural cycles, cultivating an expectation that desires can be immediately satisfied with the mere push of a button.

During my high school years, Queen entered my life. At that time, I did not know much English. My education had been French-focused, and the only English I had encountered was a weekend course in my neighbourhood during the fifth grade of elementary school. The first phrase taught was "good afternoon", which I struggled to pronounce, and I did not pursue English further. However, my enjoyment of Queen's songs made me eager to understand Freddie Mercury's lyrics, though the internet did not exist then. We used vinyl records. My first task was to locate a shop where I could transfer these vinyls onto cassette. Then I needed to access the lyrics. The only library in Ankara that held Queen's records was in the British Embassy, known as British Culture. As a boarding school student, I could only visit this library on Saturday mornings. I painstakingly transcribed the lyrics of songs (which I did not understand) into a notebook with a pencil. During the week, I would look up each word in a dictionary, translate them, and sing along to the songs, interpreting them through the meanings my translations evoked. It took me six months to fully comprehend my two favourite Queen albums.

Now, consider how this process has evolved. Not only can I instantly access the works, lyrics, and translations in any language of globally popular artists, but I can also discover any local artist from anywhere in the world within seconds. However, my brain still requires time to grasp the nuances of that language and integrate meaning into the overall process.

Of course, there is an enormous economic dimension in the background of this instant gratification. Global giant companies, capital markets, and incredible intellectual power make resistance futile. How Trendyol and Getir became some of Turkey's most valuable companies is illustrative of this dynamic. Even Getir, just before the pandemic, was about to shut down if not for securing new funding just in time. Even the right product or service at the right moment, despite seeming to be increasing the quality of our life, may end up causing damage to our psychology and ecosystem just because of the immediacy of meeting these needs. Although technology may solve the resource issue with new energy sources, distribution algorithms, and transportation methods, the impact of this process on human psychology should not be overlooked. Unless we are in harmony with ourselves, the nature and ecosystem we are part of, and unless we align with the harmonious rhythm of life, it seems unlikely that we can maintain our resilience and sustain this lifestyle.

In my elementary school years, a teacher of mine defined intelligence as the "ability to adapt". I think we often circle back to the lessons from our elementary years. With all these changes and redesigned lifestyles, it is crucial to define our main purpose in life clearly. Despite all external influences, we should strive to fulfil this main purpose by resisting evolving conditions to a certain extent. However, when a threshold is crossed, adapting to new external influences in the most appropriate and effective way for our life purpose becomes essential. Being able to make the most of the only life we have – despite all the challenges, losses, fears, worries, and even despair – by continuously embracing life without giving up and by developing strategies and taking action to succeed repeatedly, is probably our most valuable treasure.

The concept of resilience reminds us that we should develop our reflexes and strategies today, dig our wells before we become thirsty, and address important matters before they become urgent.

Change Management, Gestalt, and Coaching

While the concept of inclusion is readily articulated, truly internalizing it proves significantly more challenging, as you might agree upon by the time you reach this section. To increase our capacity for inclusion, a heightened awareness and transformation across various facets – from the psychological foundations underpinning our personality and character to our conscious and unconscious choices and biases – are required. We face formidable barriers, not only our prejudices and individual and societal patterns but also our cultural teachings and privileges – hard-earned and carefully maintained – that define us and the paradigms of the world we inhabit. These constitute obstacles, predominantly the teachings, patterns, and choices that have shaped our place, status, and lifestyle within our current society. However, I hope we can agree that our current position is not ideal. Especially due to technological and demographic reasons, we must evolve into a place where we live in harmony with those who are different from us, creating common values together. This transition requires not merely a change but a transformation. Many attributes that brought us to this point are now becoming barriers, even making our lives miserable and depriving us of many new opportunities.

How will we accomplish this change?

The most practical, simplest, and effective method at our disposal is coaching. This discussion is not intended to provide comprehensive training on coaching but rather to share a summary of the basic principles of coaching before discussing its applications.

In his book *The Inner Game of Tennis*, Tim Gallwey suggests that a tennis player simultaneously engages in two matches. If a player cannot succeed in the match within his own mind, he cannot fully realize his potential against his opponent on the court. Thus, the friction we create within ourselves essentially reveals the gap between our potential and our performance. Coaching, although unfortunately named, actually aims to increase an individual's awareness of any issue within, to clearly determine what they truly want with this heightened awareness, and to act in the direction they choose by identifying new alternatives, obstacles, and supportive resources. The term "coaching" is unfortunate because, historically in English, it refers to a horse-drawn carriage or a bus service that transports you from one place to another. In our language, this term is also associated with an animal. Moreover, particularly in sports, it is commonly used to describe someone who knows the strategy, decides it, and makes players play according to that strategy. There is also an unfortunate use of terms regarding how to name someone receiving coaching. It is incorrectly translated to "client" sometimes, which is misleading as often, another institution or person, paying for the service, sponsors and supports the individual receiving coaching. Therefore, I prefer to call the individual receiving coaching a "coachee".

After this detailed introduction, let us touch on some teachings and principles that lie at the foundation of coaching.

Coaching primarily focuses on what remains after the events in our lives and how we live onwards with the sediments left behind, rather than focusing primarily on the events themselves. It emphasizes how individuals can actively influence the occurrences in their lives, steering away from passivity or victimhood.

Coaching is concerned with the present moment. Change transpires in the here and now. It addresses the current reflections of all we have lived through, memories, lived experiences, and the future's worries, expectations, and hopes.

Imagine a triangle where the coach is at the top, the coachee at the bottom left, and the topic at the bottom right. Coaching concentrates on the edge of the triangle that represents the relationship between the coachee and the topic. The objective is not to resolve the coachee or the topic but to focus on "What is happening so that this topic out of all is now presenting itself as an issue for the coachee?"

Coaching consistently aims to enhance the coachee's awareness regarding the topic and to develop new perspectives. Expressions like "either this or that", recurring patterns, or emotions and thought patterns of unknown origins all invariably provide clues. The objective is the coachee's awareness; hence, from the coach's perspective, there is not a problem awaiting solution. Traditional problem-solving habits of "find the missing information, solve the problem" can undermine coaching. The coach must recognize that there are no clues to uncover and no problems to resolve. The overarching goal is for the coachee to become aware of their relationship with the topic. Consequently, closed-ended questions are unhelpful. The most beneficial questioning pattern is "what" though questions like "where", "when", "who", and "how" also effectively heighten the coachee's awareness and foster new insights. The questioning pattern to avoid is "why". Why? Because questions with a "why" tend to induce a defensive response. Queries such as "Why are you late?", "Why did you wear that?", and

"Why did you eat that?" implicitly suggest that being late is wrong, the attire chosen is inappropriate, or the food preference was poor. Such implications make the coachee feel judged and defensive, thus obstructing the coaching process.

In coaching, while we aim to facilitate change, the pursuit is not for those fleeting "aha" moments of awareness. The focus is not on the coach receiving accolades or nurturing their ego but on effecting a substantive change within the coachee, whether during the session or within subsequent interactions. Unlike aiming for actionable plans or cognitive outcomes, the true objective lies in catalysing change on an emotional level. Thus, we engage directly with our emotions, locating where they manifest in our bodies, giving a voice to these feelings and their physical expressions.

A key objective in coaching also involves giving a voice to stakeholders who are typically unheard or unseen within the system. A notable technique employed by Jeff Bezos, which has drawn considerable attention, involves placing an empty chair at the meeting table. This chair represents stakeholders not present, prompting discussions around how decisions might impact these absent parties. This method, symbolized through the empty chair, is frequently utilized in coaching to ensure all potential impacts are considered.

Moreover, the foundational principles of coaching necessitate a non-judgemental and non-directive approach. Here, an empathetic stance is paramount, one of the most critical skills in coaching. We have discussed empathy at length previously, so I will not delve into it again here, but it is essential to emphasize that empathy in coaching involves striving to understand another's feelings and experiences without judgement, carefully avoiding shifts towards sympathy or antipathy. In other words, cognitive empathy, not emotional, serves us in coaching.

In coaching practices, we benefit from various psychological schools and models. Cognitive psychology, positive psychology, transactional analysis, and Gestalt are the areas from which I benefit the most.

Here, since our topic involves undergoing a change and even a transformation to increase our inclusion capacity, I would like to summarize how useful coaching dialogues, starting from the Gestalt school, may be for us.

Gestalt therapy, since its introduction globally in the 1950s, first found its use in management development programmes during the 1960s through the efforts of Nevis and Wallen. Initially referred to as sensitivity training, this method employed techniques designed to enhance personal development and awareness among executives. While its foundational principles evolved into the domain of emotional intelligence development, the utilization of the Gestalt approach in fostering personal growth persists to this day, maintaining its original structure and objectives.

Subsequent to its adoption in management training, Nevis, alongside colleagues from the Cleveland Gestalt Institute in the United States, further refined Gestalt theory and its application to institutional change and consulting processes. This expansion led to the global dissemination of Gestalt practices through international training programmes, impacting hundreds, if not thousands, of senior organizational development professionals. In 1987, Nevis's publication, *Organizational Consulting: A Gestalt Approach*, articulated the core tenets of the Gestalt methodology as it applies to consulting, systemic change, and organizational development.

During this period, Sonia Nevis and Joseph Zinker extended the use of Gestalt theory to relational dynamics, applying it to couples and families under what became known as the Cape Cod model. This model fostered a systemic approach to relationship therapy. Drawing on the foundational work of the Cleveland Gestalt Institute, numerous practitioners trained under this model – including myself – have adapted Gestalt principles for use in public institutions, corporate settings, and management development initiatives. Today, the Gestalt method serves as a primary supporting theory and a cornerstone theoretical and practical framework for senior executive coaching, team development, and larger group interventions.

More recently, the application of Gestalt in senior executive coaching has grown, focusing significantly on the role of coaches as effective change agents within transformation processes. This segment of coaching emphasizes intervention strategies that are informed by Gestalt principles, which will be explored further here, sharing foundational concepts that guide coaches in navigating complex change dynamics.

Fundamental propositions of Gestalt are as follows:

- The occurrence of change and the meaning of resistance
- Awareness and change
- Perspectives on the "here" and "now"
- The experience cycle
- Working on unfinished business
- Using the self as an agent of change

But before all these, let us discuss what "Gestalt" actually means.

Whenever I commence mentoring a new cohort of coaches, I pose a question about their prior knowledge of

Gestalt. I do not anticipate a uniform response because "Gestalt", a term derived from German, lacks a precise equivalent in other languages. The term typically encapsulates notions such as form, shape, and structure in various scholarly texts. However, these interpretations fall short unless one considers the holistic essence of Gestalt. Often, individuals ascribe more significance to the term than is warranted, though few of these expanded definitions withstand rigorous scrutiny.

According to a definition by Clarkson (2004):

"The aim of the Gestalt approach is for the person to discover, explore and experience his or her own shape, pattern and wholeness. Analysis may be a part of the process but the aim of Gestalt is the integration of all disparate parts. In this way people can let themselves become totally what they already are, and what they potentially can become".

Particularly relevant are the concepts of being and becoming, which are pivotal to understanding what coaching truly involves.

Central to Gestalt are several crucial assertions about the nature of human function and the dynamics of change. Many foundational principles of coaching resonate closely with these assertions.

- Awareness precipitates change.
- The goal of the coach is to help clients become aware of their own processes (operations).
- This heightened awareness sharpens understanding of necessities and available choices and fosters more effective decision-making and actions.

- Enhanced awareness fosters a sense of personal owner-ship and accountability.
- Our needs, both emerging and predominant, shape our perception.
- We inherently perceive our environment as a com-plete whole and feel compelled to address and resolve challenges.
- There is an innate drive to endow our perceptions and experiences with meaning.
- Learning manifests through an examination of experi-ences in the context of the "here" and "now".

As underscored at the outset of this discourse, the pri-mary goal of coaching is not to transport the coachee to a predetermined destination; such an endeavour would only encounter amplified resistance. This is known as the **para-dox of change**, a principle articulated by Beisser in 1970, which is integral to the Gestalt framework.

This principle claims that before any change can occur, an individual must fully experience their present situation and reality. Beisser maintained that while individuals might strive to transform into someone they are not, their core self remains unchanged. The foundational tenet of Gestalt asserts that true change unfolds spontaneously when an individual fully acknowledges and understands their current reality. Perls, a pioneer of Gestalt therapy, suggested in 1969 that mere awareness itself holds therapeutic value.

Gallwey explains this powerful concept by putting for-ward the idea that the first step is to simply observe our cur-rent performances without either judging or trying to improve it and that paradoxically, the thing that provides the incentive and capacity for spontaneous change is the person's conscious acceptance of themselves and their actions.

Building on this concept, the exploration of how change transpires carries profound implications and often contradicts common perceptions. Whether aware of it or not, individuals frequently dismiss alternative viewpoints in favour of their own, leading to frustration, annoyance, and disillusionment when others fail to respond as anticipated.

If we accept that change is inherently challenging, it is crucial to acknowledge that people will harbour mixed feelings about it. While they may recognize its advantages, they predominantly grapple with its costs and losses, leading to a waning confidence in their capacity to change.

Kegan and Lahey, in their book, *How the Way We Talk Can Change the Way We Work* (2000), illuminate resistance to change with a poignant reflection:

> The late William Perry, a favorite teacher and precious colleague of ours at Harvard, was a gifted trainer of therapists, counselors, consultants. "Whenever someone comes to me for help," he used to say, "I listen very hard and ask myself, what does this person really want and what will they do to keep from getting it?" (. . .) As Bill's wry words suggest, if we want deeper understanding of the prospect of change, we must pay closer attention to our own powerful inclinations not to change.

From this angle, resistance is not merely an obstacle but a profoundly meaningful force that actually simplifies our tasks. To paddle against the current is futile; rather, we should embrace and value resistance as a form of creative expression and adaptation. In a context devoid of resistance, individuals would be vulnerable to manipulation and exploitation.

If we genuinely believe in showing respect to people, we must also allow them to make their own decisions and find their paths. This principle is not only foundational to Gestalt philosophy but also to the essence of coaching. A coach's role is to aid individuals in discovering who they are, what they desire, what they need, how they can enhance their productivity, and how they can satisfy these needs.

Zinker (1994) succinctly summarizes the paradoxes of change:

> If you support what is, and not what should be, change will take place. If you support resistance to change, little resistance will be encountered and change will take place.

Considerations for the Change Process

- What kind of change are we experiencing? What is changing?
- An open team with sincerity and clear intentions accelerates and democratizes change.
- What is the most challenging aspect of the change process for me?
- Creating awareness is fundamentally about open agreement in the development area.
- Which behaviours of my team members and employees do I see as resistance during this process?
- Occasionally, mental change does not manifest in behaviour.

- What factors cause me to perceive these behaviours as resistance?
- What old habits cause anxiety of the known?
- What might they see as potential threats that cause them to show resistance?
- The belief that their current success is obtained in this manner and the principle that the bird in the hand is better than two in the bush make them somewhat conservative.
- If I were to view this resistance as feedback, what could I learn to revise and improve my change efforts?
- What does the resistance I show tell me?
- To what values or purposes might this resistance be serving?

Attitudes and the notions that maintain the status quo feel safer.

Paradox of Change

In essence:

If you work with resistance and eliminate it, change occurs because the resistance itself ends up dissolving. Consider, what am I resisting and what do I tend to exclude? If I find it challenging to include, I must address this resistance. Whatever fears and anxieties I harbour, they require acknowledgement and engagement.

Take, for instance, a scenario where I struggle to feel comfortable working with a colleague who cannot use their right arm due to an illness. There is an internal block, something that challenges my values and stirs anxieties and concerns. If I fail to recognize and address these feelings, no matter how hard I try to overcome them, my discomfort may be perceptible to my colleague. They might feel unwelcome or uncomfortable. Inclusion is fundamentally about feelings; once that feeling of inclusion is compromised, no action can rectify the situation fully.

To illustrate, I recall a personal experience from about 10 to 15 years ago during a meeting of an international association in Türkiye – a setting I cherished and where I felt appreciated among young people and lively social interactions. Then, I noticed a woman wearing a headscarf. Initially, I did not engage with her, but eventually, we found ourselves seated next to each other. As we conversed, a meaningful dialogue unfolded. She was from a Middle Eastern country and had played a pivotal role in establishing that association in her homeland. This encounter led me to introspection. I questioned myself, "What was it within me that initially prevented me from approaching her, yet later facilitated a helpful interaction when I discovered her background?" This self-inquiry is crucial for overcoming personal biases and beginning to include. By confronting and resolving my anxieties, I am able to open up and embrace inclusion.

Indeed, acquiring these skills and attaining this awareness are crucial, yet implementing them effectively in life is another challenge. As the late Mr Kayra aptly noted, "There are subjects that take a day to learn, but a lifetime to master".

Mentoring

Mentoring is a reciprocal learning relationship where skills, knowledge, and expertise are shared between a mentor and a mentee through developmental conversations, experience sharing, and role modelling. This relationship spans diverse contexts and is a two-way, inclusive partnership that cherishes diversity and mutual learning.

Who Is a Mentor, and What Do They Do?

A mentor is defined as an individual who possesses a wealth of experiences, life lessons, and expertise in any given field. In the mentoring process, a mentor dispenses the situational wisdom acquired from their experiences to support the mentee's development.

The dynamics between a mentor and a mentee are crafted through a dialogue rooted in mutual respect, devoid of judgement, where each party accepts the other as they are. This dialogue is not about debate, negotiation, or argument but focuses on unbiased, open communication. As a social equalizer, mentoring nurtures a transformative partnership that might otherwise not materialize, enabling both individuals to evolve and change through their interaction within a defined purpose.

What Does "Mentee" Mean?

The mentee, typically less experienced in the matters at hand, sets the agenda in the mentoring process. They grow and transform through the inspiration, courage, knowledge, and experience they absorb during this engagement.

Benefits of Mentoring

Mentoring is designed to facilitate a mentee's development across various subject areas via inspiring and horizon-expanding conversations. The mentor, acting as a role model, utilizes their wisdom and network to guide the mentee. This process promotes an almost utopian societal structure, free from prejudice, where each person's experience contributes to the development of the other party, preparing them for future challenges, empowering them, and aiding them in discovering and diversifying their own resources and capabilities.

At the corporate level, crafting a mentoring programme stands out as one of the most effective and efficient safeguarding strategies. Mentoring, founded on non-judgemental dialogue, involves a knowledgeable individual using their life experiences to foster someone else's growth. This partnership emphasizes diversity and pursues mutual learning through role modelling, and a sharing of experiences, skills, expertise, and knowledge. As a tool for social equalization, mentoring enables a non-judgemental, empathetic dialogue, allowing two individuals who might not otherwise cross paths to engage in meaningful exchanges without bias, sympathy, or antipathy.

In the realm of mentoring, the process is not about debating, negotiating, or arguing but rather about embracing each other's perspectives as valid and engaging in a learning, evolving, and transformative partnership. During the experience-sharing phase, mentors present their insights not as directives but as options for consideration, often concluding with a query like "What would you say if I said this?" This approach enhances awareness and empowers the mentee to discover their own truths and paths within a relationship underscored by privacy, respect, confidentiality, mutual trust, and a commitment to avoiding conflicts of interest.

When effectively implemented in such a manner, mentoring significantly contributes to fostering an inclusive culture within any organization or society where it is applied. It is crucial to pay attention to specific elements in the design and execution of mentoring programmes to amplify the effectiveness of these individual mentoring interactions. In this context, utilizing the International Standards for Mentoring and Coaching Programs (ISMCP) framework provided by EMCC is strongly recommended.

Mentoring involves development-focused conversations, experience sharing, and role modelling between a mentor and a mentee. This relationship appreciates the diversity between the participants, aiming for two-way, mutual learning across various situational contexts (EMCC Global 2020). According to this perspective, mentoring leverages situational wisdom to foster the development of the mentee. As a mechanism for social equality, mentoring eschews debate, negotiation, and argument. Instead, mentor and mentee embark on a collaborative journey that respects their differences without attempting to persuade each other, offering a reciprocal learning opportunity where both parties can derive significant benefits.

Within this framework, different mentoring practices can be tailored. Traditionally, mentors are assumed to be more experienced, often older or more senior. However, in today's rapidly evolving technological and trend-driven landscape, functional experience takes precedence over seniority. Thus, in mentoring programmes prioritized according to specific goals, an individual's expertise in a particular subject matter is more critical than their age or hierarchical position. This shift allows for mentors who might be younger or from subsequent generations, depending on the focus of the mentoring subject. In scenarios where situational wisdom is not dependent on seniority or age, the concept commonly referred to as "reverse mentoring" is employed, where younger, less senior individuals serve as mentors, and older, more senior individuals take on the role of mentees.

Reverse Mentoring

In mentoring programmes where the mentor is younger and less senior, the term "reverse mentoring" is used. This also encourages the empowerment of young people in the mentoring process and supports more senior participants in taking on the mentee role.

In our studies, reverse mentoring often becomes prominent in areas such as technology, new lifestyle trends, new business models, contemporary consumer approaches, and enhancing the workplace effectiveness of Generations Y and Z. In this context, both the mentor and the mentee gain from the experience sharing during this process.

Benefits of Reverse Mentoring

Reverse mentoring practices are very beneficial in situations where the younger generation is actively supported to be more involved in corporate culture and management. In a sense, we witness very effective results even in culture change initiatives. In the context of the affected societies and target demographics, reverse mentoring practices stand out in mentoring projects which are aimed at adapting emerging trends, consumer preferences, modern lifestyle approaches, and new communication technologies to corporate culture.

Examples of Reverse Mentoring

In sectors dominated by conventional management philosophies, reverse mentoring practices have proven instrumental in assimilating more progressive methodologies. For example, one of the foremost banks in their respective country recognized a diminishing appeal towards the banking sector among young graduates and initiated a reverse mentoring project to attract this elusive young talent.

In this innovative project, mentors were recent graduates, having joined the bank within the past two years, while mentees comprised the bank's senior management. This initiative was not only aimed at cultural transformation and bolstering public relations but also served as a strategic branding endeavour. By the culmination of the project, senior management had gained profound insights into the preferences, trends, and philosophies favoured by the younger generation. Empowering these youthful mentors not only facilitated a dynamic exchange of ideas but also granted senior management the liberty to explore and question established norms more openly. Follow-up measures included the adoption of a casual Friday policy, exempting the requirement of ties, and the establishment of numerous new communication channels within the management sphere. Parallel initiatives were observed in some leading companies in the power sector, both in the electricity production and distribution. Another noteworthy instance occurred during the pandemic when a prominent industrial company, directly engaged with consumers, assigned young mentors to senior managers to adapt swiftly to the evolving work conditions.

Projects that position younger, less senior members as mentors not only empower these individuals but also furnish senior managers with the opportunity to engage in open observation, thereby enriching both the mentor and the mentee extensively through this process. It is imperative for both parties to engage in an unbiased, inclusive dialogue aligned with the programme's objectives. Project managers and sponsors must be particularly vigilant in this regard. To actualize these elements most effectively, it is paramount to support the project with an internationally accredited training programme, thereby adequately preparing both mentees and mentors.

Mentoring and Advice

We say there is no giving advice in mentoring. So what should be done?

Why Should We Not Give Advice in Mentoring?

Envision a scenario where offered guidance achieves the intended outcome. What transpires subsequently? The dilemma seems resolved, accolades accrue to the mentor for this triumph, yet what substantive learning or evolution has the mentee undergone? All credits go to the mentor. Conversely, consider the instance where the advice precipitates adverse results. In this case "put the blame on the mentor". The issue persists, exacerbates, and culpability is ascribed to the mentor. What enlightenment and growth does the mentee derive from this predicament?

In the mentoring paradigm, it is imperative for the mentee to shoulder responsibility and evolve through inspiration drawn from the mentor's shared experiences. That is, the overarching importance is placed on the mentee's continual development beyond the direct presence of the mentor. The essence lies not in merely resolving the issue at hand – note, we refrain from terming it a "problem" – but in enabling the mentee to achieve a deeper awareness of their relationship with the challenge. This nurtures an environment where the mentee can acquire new perspectives and draw inspiration from the experiences shared by the mentor, thereby embarking on a transformative journey.

So how should a mentor convey their thoughts that might be beneficial to the mentee or offer advice on actions the mentee should consider? What are the appropriate circumstances, timing, and methods for such exchanges?

Allowing the mentee to concentrate on crucial points – which can even be viewed from the mentor's perspective – can accelerate their development beyond their individual capabilities and maximize the benefits derived from the mentor's experiences. Nonetheless, the process of dispensing advice is fraught with considerable drawbacks. When individuals grapple with their issues independently and forge their solutions:

- They tend to embrace these solutions more wholeheartedly.
- They assume greater responsibility for the outcomes.

In mentoring, the ultimate aim is to get the mentee from a passive "victim" position and enable them with an attitude of "being in charge of their lives". This involves providing them with new perspectives, role modelling, context sharing, transfer of contextual wisdom so that they can get inspiration, energy, and enthusiasm to move on. With this in mind, avoiding giving advice in developmental mentoring proves to be more beneficial. In this context, it is imperative to augment the mentee's awareness concerning the subject matter before offering advice.

You can explore the potential possibilities in the subsequent section as we delineated the rationales for the matter at hand in the preceding section. Now, let us explore what is technically feasible here.[2]

Initially, it is essential to elucidate what mentoring entails through a well-known metaphor. Our principal objective in mentoring is not merely to provide fish or teach fishing but rather to enhance the mentee's consciousness about fish and fishing across various dimensions such as thought patterns, prejudices, attitudes, and preferences. This involves assisting them in identifying and surmounting their motivators and impediments, planning and internalizing the necessary resources to integrate these into their life. Consequently, raising the mentee's awareness about the topic of the advice prior to advancing to the advice phase holds significant importance. Essentially, curtailing the provision of advice in developmental mentoring yields greater effectiveness.

Where Does Sharing Advice Fit, and What Is Possible?

Let us state our concluding thoughts at the outset: if the intention is for the mentee to discover their solutions and to embrace a more accountable stance towards their convictions, the most fitting intervention a mentor can employ is to present the advice they wish to impart, and instead of concluding their statement with a period, they should use a comma and add, "What would you say if I said this?" thereby inviting a pause.

The objective here is for the mentee to acquire a moment for introspection, to thoroughly contemplate the advice shared, to explore how the awareness it engenders might be advantageous, and through this "reflection" or profound contemplation, to ascertain where it leads and what they derive from this engagement. What other forms of interventions might promote this approach?

Guidance is a technique that a relatively inexperienced mentor may confidently utilize only under specific conditions. Within guidance:

- The questions you pose, drawn from your own insights and knowledge, encourage the mentee to embark on a similar thought process.
- Proposing a solution is contingent upon the mentee's consent. Initially, it is imperative to ascertain whether the mentee perceives a necessity for it.

The inherent risk with guidance is that a solution effective for one mentor may not suit another. It behooves the mentor to introspect, questioning, "How pertinent are my experiences and ideas to this particular scenario?" Should there be any uncertainty, it necessitates a shift back to a non-directive approach, focusing solely on posing questions.

When Is It Appropriate to Give Advice?

The following factors will play a decisive role in this regard.

There are instances where immediate, directive advice becomes crucial. For example, if the mentee is on the brink of a significant error, the mentor is obligated to alert them to potential unseen repercussions. Yet a conscientious mentor will revisit this topic at the earliest opportunity, re-evaluate it, and ensure that the mentee derives lasting lessons from the experience.

It is essential to emphasize that our discussion pertains specifically to developmental mentoring. Unlike sponsorship mentoring, which emphasizes providing advice and guidance, developmental mentoring employs these strategies sparingly. In developmental mentoring, before deciding to offer advice or guidance on a specific issue, the mentor seeks to ensure a comprehensive understanding of the situation within its context by both parties. Typically, solutions emerge naturally for the mentee through the process of dialogue and reflective thinking, obviating the need for direct advice from the mentor. Should the need persist, the mentor may resort to offering guidance or advice as a final measure.

Here lies a pivotal consideration: the mentee should not habitually expect their mentor to formulate solutions. Once there is a robust understanding of the issue, the mentor can encourage the mentee to reflect on the problem extensively – spanning hours, days, or even weeks – before revisiting it, allowing the mentee ample time to ponder.

How Can the Mentor Be Helpful?

Questions related to this topic are as follows:

- How can offering advice or guidance aid the mentee in their immediate context and in future similar situations?
- What will constitute the range of your beneficial responses? These may include sharing advice, providing guidance, questioning, listening attentively, offering challenges, and so on.

- What motivates you to offer advice or guidance? Is it to enhance your own image or to alleviate internal tension by expressing your thoughts?
- If you were in the mentee's position, what type of intervention would you find most beneficial in the same circumstance?

The mentor ought to take a moment to consider these queries before responding to the mentee (without intervening). This reflective pause will naturally decelerate the conversation, affording the mentee an opportunity for deep contemplation, and empower the mentor to respond aptly to the mentee's needs.

Whose issue is it, really?

The more the issue is owned by the mentee, the greater the imperative for them to develop and implement their solutions.

Conditions for Sharing Advice[3]

- If the question posed by the mentee necessitates a straightforward yes/no answer, particularly in specialized areas such as legal, medical, or financial issues.
- In crisis situations requiring immediate action.
- If the mentee's physical, financial, or psychological safety is jeopardized without direct advice.
- If the mentee lacks the capacity to make informed decisions independently.
- When presenting factual information, rather than personal opinions.

- If the mentee explicitly requests specific information and intends to make their own decision on its application.
- If it is feasible to encourage the mentee to seek further opinions from other experts.
- In cases where the mentee encounters unexpected issues requiring expert guidance.
- When providing advice does not foster a dependency relationship or foster unrealistic optimism in the mentee.
- If your motivation is not one of the following:

  - Efforts to influence and show off.
  - Control.

Basic Rules for Sharing Advice

- Encourage the mentee to heed their inner guidance when considering any advice.
- If convinced that your input is necessary, seek permission from the mentee before offering advice.
- Reflect on the *reasons* for wanting to give advice. Is it genuinely to assist the mentee, or do you believe you have the best answer?
- Deliver advice clearly and specifically, distinguishing between particular and general guidance.
- Try listening to yourself while giving advice.
- Keep your advice succinct and focused.
- Ensure that the advice you give will lead to more in-depth dialogue.
- After advising, assist the mentee in integrating the advice with their personal assessments and actions.

Structuring Advice Sharing

- Explain *why* you are giving the advice.
- Identify the *source* of your advice, whether it is from personal experience, observations, intuitive feelings, information from third parties, research, and so on.
- Keep your advice brief and concise.
- Confirm that the mentee comprehends the advice as intended.
- Verify if the mentee finds the advice relevant and helpful.
- Observe how the mentee modifies the advice, adapting it to their unique situation.

Lastly, a reflective question to consider:

What measures can you take to ensure that you are not simply rushing to share your advice?

Situational Leadership

There exists a plethora of leadership models. Delving into the discourse on mentorship through a leadership lens unveils one particularly efficacious model: the "situational leadership" theory. Notably, while a myriad of leadership paradigms predominantly centre on the leader's attributes – encompassing numerous frameworks delineating the essential qualities, personality traits, priorities, and methods a leader ought to embody – the situational leadership model distinguishes itself by its emphatic focus on the leader's team members, rather than solely on the leaders.

Pioneered by Ken Blanchard and introduced into scholarly discourse, the situational leadership model commences with a critical diagnostic phase. In this phase, leaders evaluate their team members against two pivotal criteria: the extent of their knowledge, skills, and experience pertinent to the tasks they are assigned, and their motivation level to undertake these tasks. This analytical process to ascertain the specific quadrant each team member occupies within these two axes is vital for the applicability and functionality of the situational leadership model.

Blanchard's formulation of situational leadership claims that an individual may concurrently occupy different quadrants across various subjects and roles in their life. Furthermore, it acknowledges that individuals may transition between quadrants as their circumstances and roles evolve over time.

Foremost, according to situational leadership theory, it is expected that a leader's approach to their team members should be appropriate to the quadrant they occupy. Thus, in the model of situational leadership, it is not anticipated that a leader would interact with all their team members in the same manner. In this context, I would like to explain how the model works and the approaches of situational leadership by referring to those under the leader's influence as "mentees".

The support needed by individuals to progress towards a desired goal can vary. Some may need more information, while others might need a clearer vision of their goals and a better understanding of what achieving those goals entail. For some, emotional support is necessary. For other mentees, taking bold steps and learning from them might prove effective. Depending on the situation and the individual, the mentor or leader exhibits different leadership styles.

Primarily, the mentee's level of knowledge and experience, motivation to act, self-confidence, and courage must be assessed. This is precisely what we refer to by "situational".

- For a mentee who is highly motivated but lacks the necessary knowledge or experience in their field of interest, the mentor's task is to bridge this gap by sharing their own experiences and be a teacher who waits patiently for the student to learn and develop.
- When a mentee demonstrates both high competence and strong motivation, the leader should be a person who knows how to delegate, who opens up new visions and horizons for the mentee while creating a space for them to be able to progress on their own.
- A mentee might possess substantial knowledge yet exhibit a lack of motivation to advance. The leader proceeds to facilitate a discovery of what passion and inner motivation look like for the mentee. In this context,

they listen, appreciate, remind of strengths, and if necessary, offer new perspectives.

- Lastly, if a mentee is neither sufficiently motivated nor experienced in the subject matter, it is expected that the leader should be one who encourages the mentee to stay the course and continue developing. This leader should inspire and, if necessary, guide the mentee to progress, even in small steps, to take controlled risks, and to muster the courage to act. In essence, the leader is expected to be challenging, directive, and a spark igniter in guiding the mentee along this journey.

Challenges of Situational Leadership Theory

One of the foremost challenges in implementing the situational leadership model lies in the potential discord between the mentee's self-perception and the leader's assessment regarding the quadrant they belong to. For instance, a mentee might consider themselves competent, whereas their leader may not share this view. Alternatively, a mentee who believes they are eager and willing might struggle to communicate this enthusiasm to their leader. Resolving these discrepancies effectively hinges on the application of robust coaching skills. Both mentor and leader must engage in active listening and pose incisive, pertinent questions to enhance the mentee's self-awareness regarding their skills and attitudes.

Similarly, it is imperative for the mentee to employ coaching skills in their interactions with their leader. This approach helps in clarifying judgement, removing any prejudices, and fostering a more conscious perception.

Furthermore, the influence of one role on another presents an additional complexity, especially for individuals who occupy different quadrants in various aspects of their lives simultaneously. For example, a lack of willingness or low morale in one role could adversely affect their performance or demeanour in another role. This misalignment might lead to misjudgements by those they interact with in different contexts. Here too, the remedy involves bolstering individual self-awareness, which is best achieved through engaging in coaching conversations that are rich in skilful questioning and reflective listening.

For those navigating their professional and personal growth both as mentees and leaders, situational leadership offers substantial advantages. To gain a deeper understanding and more effectively internalize the principles of situational leadership, delving into Ken Blanchard's concise yet insightful work, *The One Minute Manager*,[4] is highly recommended.

Fiedler's Situational Leadership Model

Another leadership paradigm that places a strong emphasis on situational contexts is the model proposed by Fiedler. This model explores the dynamics of leader-member relations, asserting that mutual respect, trust, and even affection play crucial roles in the effectiveness of leadership between leaders and their subordinates. Central to this theory is the notion of the leader's positional power, which hinges on the acceptance of the leaders' role by team members. Fiedler's model claims that the efficacy of leadership is inherently tied to the environment – the fit between the leader's style and the situational demands. Accordingly, leaders are more likely to excel in environments that align with their natural management style, whether it be task-oriented or relationship-focused, which consequently enhances the overall group performance.

The Four Horsemen of the Apocalypse

World-renowned therapists John and Julie Gottman have made significant contributions to the field of human psychology through their extensive research on couples. They have identified what they call the "Four Horsemen of the Apocalypse" in communication patterns, a metaphor derived from the New Testament by the Gottmans, where the Four Horsemen herald the end of times. And in the context of relationships, these patterns are seen as predictors of failure.

Since the 1970s, the Gottmans and their research team have studied thousands of couples, discovering that certain destructive behaviours can cause irreparable harm to relationships. While it is common for people to occasionally fall into these negative patterns, the key is to recognize and gradually overcome them to prevent lasting damage to our romantic partnerships, as well as our interactions with colleagues and within our broader social circles.

And here are these Four Horsemen that are causing damage to our relationships:

- Criticism
- Defensiveness
- Contempt
- Stonewalling

Why is it important to consider the Four Horsemen in the context of inclusion? Inclusion, both in its definition and philosophy, hinges on the establishment of robust social relationships. The foundation of such relationships is the enhancement of communication via positive, non-detrimental, and accurate language. Steering clear of the

"Four Horsemen" constitutes an essential initial step towards fostering and maintaining healthy communication within institutions or teams.

Suggestions for Surviving the Rapture

Criticism   Criticism is the first to emerge among the destructive Four Horsemen of relationships. It manifests as the tendency to verbally attack your partner's character or to blame them for the imperfections you perceive in your life.

You may find yourself using absolutes like "never", "always", and "all the time", when addressing an issue. The key distinction between criticism and expressing discomfort lies in the focus on the problem itself. For instance, if you return home exhausted and are upset by the disorder in the kitchen, stating "This is a disheartening scene" offers a constructive approach to the issue. Conversely, if you exclaim, "You don't care about me. Look at the state of this kitchen!" you initiate a cycle of mutual stress and conflict.

The more pointed and harsh your initial communication, the more likely it is to continue in that manner. Opting for deescalating such situations in your interactions can alleviate the tension for the other party.

- Inform your partner or team member about what is bothering you.
- Do not shy away from expressing your emotions.
- Articulate your requirements regarding the situation that troubles you.

Example: "Why are you always late getting ready?"
Suggestion: Gentle start-up.
State how you feel about the situation and what you need.
"I'm stressed because we're late. We need to be on time".

Defensiveness Defensiveness is characterized by a sense of victimization used to ward off a perceived attack or to shift the blame. It often emerges as a response to criticism, thus defining defensiveness may involve developing a strategy to counter such criticism. When individuals become defensive, they typically resort to methods such as the following:

- Over-explaining
- Playing the victim
- Retaliating
- Initiating arguments with "but" or "however"

Employing these methods might lead to misunderstandings, even if you are justified in your position. Every defensive reaction causes the other party to feel unheard, potentially escalating their criticisms. While everyone has the right to voice their thoughts and feelings in response to criticism, it is crucial to learn how to do so appropriately and timely. This involves listening to the other person and acknowledging our own errors and shortcomings.

Example: "Come on, you know I have trouble getting up in the morning!"

Suggestion: Taking responsibility.

Recognize your partner's viewpoint and apologize for any misconduct. This acknowledgement is a fundamental element of a healthy relationship.

"I'm sorry I was late. I know being on time is important to you".

Contempt Contempt is identified as assaulting your partner's self-esteem with disdainful or injurious language, indicating a sense of superiority. It is the most perilous of the Horsemen. According to Gottman's research, contempt is the strongest predictor of divorce.

Excessive criticism may border on contempt and is often expressed through sarcastic comments.

Example: "I learned how to tell the time when I was five years old. Let's see when you'll be able to learn".

Suggestion: Instead of concentrating on your partner's faults, express your positive needs and do not hesitate to demonstrate appreciation. This is a crucial reinforcement in a relationship. Studies suggest that positive interactions should occur five times more frequently than negative ones to maintain a healthy relationship dynamic.

"Being punctual is important for me. It would be nice if you accommodated me on this matter".

Stonewalling and Building Walls in Relationships
Stonewalling, or setting boundaries in a relationship, also referred to as "walling", is defined as withdrawing from interaction to avoid conflict and to signify disapproval, distance, and separation. Building walls in a relationship can make the other person feel neglected.

The physical demeanour of someone who is stonewalling might provide clues, such as avoiding eye contact, crossing arms over the chest, or suddenly falling silent. This behaviour is closely linked to feeling threatened. When faced with a threat, the body may react with survival instincts such as freezing, fleeing, or fighting. Under such conditions, it is difficult to think constructively about resolving issues. We lose the capacity to smile, lighten the atmosphere, or show compassion.

Example: "I can't take this anymore. I need to get out of here".

Suggestion: Calm yourself down. Employ a pre-agreed signal or word to request a pause. Use this break to partake in a soothing activity alone.

"Break! I need a break. I'm going for a walk. We can talk again in 30 minutes".[5]

It is important to note that it takes approximately 20 minutes for stress hormones to be flushed out through circulation. Engaging in minor activities during this time can aid in alleviating stress hormones.

Additionally,

- Engage in breathing exercises.
- Take a brisk walk.
- Perform simple physical exercises.
- Refrain from ruminating on the argument and perpetuating it in your thoughts.

You may be contemplating how to rectify the disruptions caused by the Four Horsemen. We all occasionally fall into using one or several of these destructive communication patterns. Fortunately, it is possible to repair this damage if you are committed. Should you wish to heal and improve the situation:

- If you recognize one of the Horsemen in either your own or another's speech, initiate the conversation anew using different expressions. Should you find yourself employing them, be certain to offer an apology.
- Should the situation escalate, adopt behaviours that infuse warmth into the relationship, such as utilizing humour, extending apologies, or demonstrating curiosity.
- Endeavour to thoroughly understand the Four Horsemen and enhance your interpersonal skills.

- Learn to articulate specific grievances and requests such as "When X occurred, I felt as if Y and I would like some Z at the moment".
- Develop conscious communication.
- Convey your grasp of the other person's perspective; ensure they are aware that you comprehend their emotions and can empathize with their viewpoint.
- Reframe your internal dialogue, substituting thoughts of justifiable rage or passive victimhood with sentiments of gratitude, reassurance, and accountability.
- Embrace vulnerability, accept your partner's remarks as mere expressions – thoughts and ephemeral words – and relinquish any preconceived narratives you hold.

Mini Test

Love and admiration are crucial components of a successful long-term relationship. Regular demonstrations of mutual appreciation make it significantly easier to handle stressful periods and to resolve conflicts. To gauge the level of love and admiration in your relationship, consider taking a brief assessment based on questions devised by Dr John Gottman.[6]

I can easily list the three things about my partner that I admire the most.

True / False

☐ ☐

When apart, I frequently think of my partner with affection.

True / False

☐ ☐

I make it a point to often say "I love you" to my partner.

True / False

☐ ☐

I frequently express affection through touch or kisses.

True / False

☐ ☐

My partner genuinely respects me.

True / False

☐ ☐

I feel loved and appreciated in this relationship.

True / False

☐ ☐

I am truly proud of my partner.

True / False

☐ ☐

My partner actively celebrates my successes and achievements.

True / False

☐ ☐

We seldom go to sleep without expressing love or affection.

True / False

☐ ☐

My spouse values the contributions I make to our marriage.

True / False

☐ ☐

Advice for a Data Scientist

The world we inhabit gravitates towards a technology-driven, data-centric era, so let us have a look at an article designed to inspire us all – youth and those who remain youthful in spirit alike – under the banner: Advice for the future data scientist.[7,8]

Topics:

1. Be curious.
2. Do not forget the "science" in data science.
3. Be aware of how others perceive you.
4. Know what you are working with.
5. Be aware of the hypes.
6. Tell a story.
7. Acquire a T-shaped proficiency.
8. Be Pareto-efficient.
9. Learn for the sake of learning.
10. Have a growth mindset.
11. Challenge your own ideas.
12. Be aware of the changing world.

Be Curious

If you do not identify as a curious individual, this profession may not suit you. The realm of data is replete with marvels, though not invariably. Consider data mining as a fitting metaphor: one must sift through copious amounts of debris and dust to uncover the valuable ore. And as a wise man once said:

- All that glitters is not gold.
- It is akin to embarking on a maritime adventure.

- How does the world function?
- How do these new technologies operate?
- What do the data convey?
- What direction is the world headed?

Should you let curiosity guide you, you are bound to eventually encounter the promised wonders and riches. The sage further remarked:

- Not all who wander are lost.

Do Not Forget the "Science" in Data Science

The allure of shiny, novel technologies is ever-present, with new advancements arriving daily – from all these attention models to GANs and from feature pyramids to memory networks and proximity policy optimizations. One might easily be tempted to employ these to address the task at hand.

However, the "science" aspect of data science often plays the overlooked, younger sibling within the family. Embracing the principles of the scientific method will likely aid you more than anticipated.

Approach your endeavours as scientific projects whenever feasible. Remember to incorporate elements like hypothesis testing and maintain a stance of scientific scepticism. At times, the most formidable adversary to the success of your model could be your own biases – biases that might even infiltrate your data or your models.

Perhaps now is a good time to recount the tale of John Snow – not the character you might be thinking of but the real John Snow, who is arguably the world's first data scientist.

It was the year 1854. London lacked a sewage system, and a cholera outbreak was wreaking havoc with deadly consequences. During this era, germ theory had not yet been accepted, and prevailing belief attributed disease to miasma or bad air. The common countermeasures – pleasant aromas – proved utterly ineffective, and the mortality rates soared. Enter John Snow. Setting aside the prevailing theories of his era, he turned to his data for answers and started to meticulously mark all the cholera cases on a map, but no, they were not random at all!

He formed a hypothesis that it had something to do with the water. And when the wells near the heavily infected population were shut down, the outbreak finally subsided.

The lesson from the story is, if you are sceptical about what people have to say, are willing to look at the data, and have a hypothesis that you can test, then you might just end up saving many lives.

Be Aware of How Others Perceive You

Knowing how others perceive you can wield considerable influence. It allows you to strategize your approach towards them or anticipate their expectations.

For customers, you are perceived as a spoiled child wielding a powerful laser gun. They surmise that most of your capabilities are simply due to you possessing this advanced tool, and if they had it, they might achieve similar results as well. However, they are way too preoccupied for experiments. Get used to encountering remarks such as "This is just machine learning", "This is just statistics", or "I read an article recently about what they could do".

For your non-data scientist co-workers, you often appear as a magician. The tasks you accomplish seem bizarre to them, and because you can achieve these feats, they might expect further miracles from you. Thus, for many, the nature of your work and your methods remain enigmatic.

For human resources, you are a unicorn. There are some rumours that unicorns exist. Of course, they work hard to find one, and sometimes they are disappointed when they see it. Because, as it turns out, you are not some magical beast.

Of course, these clichés are not always true or might even be a bit mixed up. In any case, it is crucial to communicate with an awareness of how one is perceived. It may be wise to steer clear of reinforcing certain misconceptions while striving to dismantle others.

Know What You Are Working With

Know what you are working with. It is essential to understand the technologies you utilize intimately. Take time, for instance, to grasp how TensorFlow operates or why CNNs excel with image data. Deeply explore the domain in which you operate.

Emulate the child who not only plays with his toys but also disassembles them to see how they work, sometimes causing them to break.

While a conceptual understanding of your tools is necessary, mastering the mathematical underpinnings can provide you with what feels like a superpower.

Be Aware of the Hypes

Deep learning and other cutting-edge technologies are not fraudulent, but their potential can be overstated. The field of AI and neural network research has seen its fair share of highs and lows, accompanied by unrealistic expectations that sometimes fall short. As revolutionary as these technologies are, they may, in fact, not be the panacea for all the challenges we face.

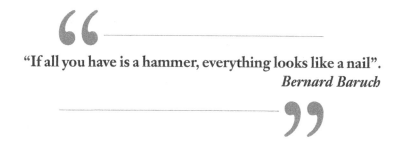

"If all you have is a hammer, everything looks like a nail".
Bernard Baruch

Do not let the models you have become a hammer. Some days the optimal solution could even be a logistic regression.

Tell a Story

We are definitely proud of our technical achievements. There are few things that could be better than solving a tough problem. However, solving real-life problems unfortunately has non-technical aspects as well.

When working with data, we utilize error functions to gauge our performance, continuously seeking optimization. Unfortunately, the error functions do not measure how useful our model is or how successful it appears to be. Predicting results with good accuracy may not just cut it.

Not everyone will be swayed by accuracy, error measurements, or confusion matrices because you are not speaking their language.

Stories, however, are universally understood. Frame your results, provide scenarios, and narrate stories to help others grasp what you are doing. Incorporate striking visualizations for added impact. Remember, your role is not just about data – it inevitably involves interacting with others.

Acquire a T-Shaped Proficiency

It is beneficial to have a broad knowledge base, as you cannot always predict the nature of the problems you will encounter. Often, the solution involves a mix of very different things.

Moreover, specialize in at least one area. This specialization not only allows you to solve certain problems that many cannot but also demonstrates your capacity to achieve and repeat your success, a valuable trait and an overlooked side effect with regard to your career.

Be Pareto-Efficient

Building a model is like shopping online. By spending a little more money, you can always find something better. Better, repeat a little bit more again. But then, you are now way beyond your budget. Similarly, yes, you can always spend more time making your models better. Repeat a little bit more.

The Pareto principle can instruct us at this point, as the 80% of the results come from 20% of our efforts. Focusing on this crucial 20% can maximize our efficiency and the effectiveness of our work.

Though it is often inevitable to focus on the 20% of results, being mindful of which part you dedicate effort to always proves beneficial. Constantly contemplate how you might achieve superior results with the time you allocate.

Learn for the Sake of Learning

"Give me six hours to chop down a tree and I will spend the first four sharpening the ax".

Abraham Lincoln

Each minute you specifically devote to solving a problem is expended on that very problem. Similarly, the time you invest in learning the details of the latest technologies will predominantly benefit you in that area. Attempting to understand these without the appropriate foundational knowledge is akin to attempting to cut down a tree with a dull axe.

The time spent on developing your fundamental and theoretical knowledge might not directly yield a solution to a specific problem. Nevertheless, the stronger your foundational knowledge, the quicker you can learn new information. This is analogous to sharpening your axe.

Furthermore, mastering the art of learning itself can significantly speed up the process of acquiring new knowledge and skills. This enhancement is comparable to refining your grinding stone, which subsequently reduces the time needed for each session of axe sharpening. So what is the recommended course of action? Broaden your exposure to a variety of subjects – not exclusively technical ones – immerse yourself in extensive reading, and maintain openness to novel ideas.

Have a Growth Mindset

In this field, you will find yourself collaborating, at least virtually, with some of the most brilliant minds of your era. Some of these individuals may indeed be geniuses. Tasks that you find challenging may seem effortless to them. Inevitably, you will find yourself drawing comparisons with these peers. At times, such comparisons may lead you to feel inadequate. However, it is important to remember that this feeling is widespread and commonly known as imposter syndrome.

The encouraging reality is that you do not need to be the preeminent figure in your field; rather, being competent and effective in problem-solving suffices. Individuals across various domains universally aspire to this level of proficiency.

As noted previously, you will indeed face challenges and sometimes feel inadequate. However, embracing a growth mindset is a pivotal characteristic that distinguishes those who find success in academic and professional settings.

When setbacks occur, some individuals perceive these as limits to their intellectual capacity and consequently shift their focus to other pursuits. They resign themselves to the belief that they were not inherently suited for the tasks at hand. In contrast, those who adopt a growth mindset recognize that limitations are not solely dictated by innate capacity. They understand that their cognitive abilities are malleable. Given adequate time and systematic effort, they are capable of mastering concepts that initially appeared daunting. This is likely a scenario you will encounter when engaging with academic literature. Initially, comprehension may be challenging, but persistence leads to greater ease over time. It is essential to recognize that your mind is adaptable and capable of expansion.

Challenge Your Own Ideas

This relates to critical thinking and scientific scepticism. It is substantially easier and more effective to critique your own ideas and models before they face the scrutiny of data or the critiques from others.

In essence, I am offering the same advice Lord Petyr Baelish gave to Sansa.[9]

> Do not fight in the North or the South. Fight every battle everywhere, always, in your mind. Everyone is your enemy, everyone is your friend. Every possible series of events is happening all at once. Live that way and nothing will surprise you. Everything that happens will have been something you've seen before.

Be Mindful of the Changing World

With the advent of the steam engine and the ensuing Industrial Revolution, the erstwhile predominance of human muscle power dwindled. Machines, far surpassing human strength and devoid of fatigue, took centre stage. Consequently, the most precious attribute of our species became our intellect – the capacity to learn, think, calculate, and resolve complex problems. Today, this very facet of our being faces unprecedented challenges.

Interestingly, we, as the mentors of these machines, play a part in this evolution. At times, I reflect on the human labour that gave rise to the steam engine. The workers were essentially crafting a technology that diminished their immediate utility, yet simultaneously, they were forging a tool that would benefit humanity at large.

Our engagement with cognitive science, coupled with our insights into psychology and neuroscience, suggests that we are still distinct from machines in significant ways. Machines excel in areas that challenge us yet falter in tasks that we navigate with ease. Consider, for instance, how humans outperform in certain computer games, but in turn, remember that artificial intelligence was able to beat the games themselves.

Thus, it is crucial to discern precisely what computers excel at and where human proficiency remains superior. Avoid dedicating excessive effort to tasks that machines can perform effortlessly, such as complex numerical computations. Strive not to become merely another cog in the machinery of this new era.

Notes

1. On this matter, I wholeheartedly recommend the study *The Athena Doctrine: How Women (and the Men Who Think Like Them) Will Rule the Future* by John Gerzema and Michael D'Antonio. The methodology and findings of the study were impeccably summarized by Gerzema at TEDxKC.
2. This article was inspired by the works of D. Clutterbuck on this topic.
3. The following checklist is quoted from Jenny Roger's *Coaching Skills* handbook.
4. Ken Blanchard and Spencer Johnson, *The One Minute Manager*, Harper Collins UK, 2011.
5. Dr John M. Gottman and Dr Julie Schwartz Gottman.
6. https://www.gottman.com/blog/fondness-and-admiration-assessment
7. https://obss.tech/en/https-medium-com-codable-advice-for-a-future-data-scientist-81e1caa6fe9e
8. https://obss.tech/en/https-medium-com-codable-advice-for-a-future-data-scientist-81e1caa6fe9e/
9. Game of Thrones

Index